ANGOLA IN THE BLACK CULTURAL EXPRESSIONS OF BRAZIL

ANGOLA IN THE BLACK CULTURAL EXPRESSIONS OF BRAZIL

GERHARD KUBIK

DIASPORIC AFRICA PRESS

This book is a publication of

DIASPORIC AFRICA PRESS
New York | www.dafricapress.com

ISBN-13 978-1-937306-10-6 (pbk.: alk paper)
Library of Congress Control Number: 2013956649

CONTENTS

PREFACE

The transplantation of African musical cultures to the Americas was a multi-track and multi-time process. In the past many historical studies of African diaspora music, dance and other aspects of expressive culture concentrated on events in the Americas. What happened before the American trauma and simultaneously in Africa was often looked at unhistorically. Excessive stability with regard to cultures in Black Africa was often silently assumed. While the fact of a changing continuity in African cultural expressions on the mother continent was mostly ignored, the impact of Western cultures on the African populations in America was often magnified. The content of African diaspora music history was understood basically in terms of *acculturation*. On the African continent the search concentrated on "roots."

In my own approach I am unable to perceive African music merely as the "roots" of something else. I consider African music and dance forms as the products of people living in various African cultures which have changed continuously in history, absorbing and processing elements from inside and outside the continent, creating new styles and fashions all the time. African diaspora music then appears as a consequent and creative *extension overseas* of African musical cultures that have existed in the period between the sixteenth and the twentieth century.

From this perspective African diaspora music cannot be described adequately in terms of "retentions" and "survivals," as if African cultures in the Americas were doomed from the outset and perhaps only by some act of mercy permitted to "retain" certain elements. In this book the term "Black Music" embraces any music showing predominance of Black African music or musical concepts and characteristics, regardless of the ethnic or racial composition of its exponents. The objective of the book, therefore, is to track down some aspects of the Angolan dimension in the panorama of African music and dance cultures in Brazil, and also to discuss methodology applicable in the wider context of African diaspora cultural studies.

AFRICAN PEOPLES AND CULTURES IN BRAZIL

Brazilian musical forms have many sources: Portuguese and other European; African from Nigeria, Dahomey, Angola, Congo (present-day Democratic Republic of the Congo) and Mozambique; and up to the more recent influences of jazz, for instance in *bossa nova,* various inter-Latin-American influences and the most recent impact of North American Rock and Soul music. Historically, there are also traces of "Arabic" or Moorish elements in some areas (particularly in the northeast). They have penetrated the Brazilian scene by way of the Iberian Peninsula or by way of West Africa.

Music in today's Brazil displays a variety of social codes. Distinctive kinds of Brazilian music are associated with social groups in a class society. Musical tastes and practices often appear as an "identification tag" for membership of certain social classes. For instance, *active* participation in *candomblé* is still a rather esoteric religious affair; street *samba* in Bahia is a popular music in the widest sense of the world, that is, the "people," mainly of the "lower" class, are the carriers of this tradition, while *bossa nova* and other more recent forms of urban *samba* have "climbed" socially in recent years and become a musical entertainment among the higher middle class inhabitants of the slender *edificios* which mark the skyline of Brazil's major cities.

The African connections of African-Brazilian musical forms are to be found mainly in two large culture areas of Black Africa: 1) Southwestern Nigeria and Benin (formerly known as Dahomey), and 2) Angola and southwestern Congo. This is a simplification, but it is a useful preliminary distinction for the identification of the main African cultures that have overseas extensions in Brazil. Besides, there are less significant African traits from Mozambique (mainly from the area of the lower Zambezi valley and the hinterland of the Northern Mozambique coast) and some western Sudanic elements originating in the broad savannah belt north of the Guinea coast. The latter are identifiable ethnically mainly as Manding (Mande) and Hausa. Some of these western Sudanic minorities used to carry on in Brazil a living tradition as trick artists and "magicians." Thus the term *mandingueros* arose, meaning "magicians" in general. In 1835, Johann Rugendas reports extensively about the activities of these western Sudanic minorities and their social place in nineteenth century Brazil.[1]

Around 1530 the systematic colonization of Brazil by Portuguese settlers began. For more than three centuries, unofficially up to the year 1888, when slavery was abolished by the dynasty of the Bragança, people from Africa were deported to Brazil. Today there is a population of over 90 million Brazilians of marked African descent.

Up to the late nineteenth century the African population was divided into "nações" (nations) on the basis of ethnic or pseudo-ethnic groupings. Though these coincided at large with actual cultural divisions in the African-Brazilian populations, they were often targeted by the authorities for political oppression. After 1888 these divisions were considered shameful and ethnic consciousness began to disappear among the Africans in Brazil.

What were called "nations" in Brazil was defined by a curious assortment of African names which were not always ethnic. "Benguela," for instance, is the name of a port in Angola from which many people were shipped to Brazil. One of the groups was mostly composed of Kirenge, Humbi, Handa, Mwila, Chipongo, Ambo, Kwisi and other ethnic divisions from the wide area of southwestern Angola. They had a similar culture and were able to communicate among themselves. So they were lumped together as one group by the slave traders. Generally the slave traders paid attention to language groupings in the African territories for reasons of commercial convenience. The result was the usage of "ethnic" designations that were in reality *trade marks* for the human "goods" to be sold. "Benguela," "Congo," "Angola," "Monjolo," etc., were labels with which the prospective buyer in Brazil associated certain qualities in appearance and character to be expected from the subjects (Figs. 1 and 2).

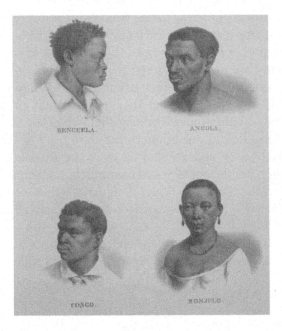

Fig. 1. Portraits of Angolans in Brazil, drawn by Johann Moritz Rugendas, 1835. "Benguela" was a designation for people who belonged to ethnic groups in southwestern, middle and eastern Angola and were shipped off through the port of Benguela. "Angola" refers to the historical Mbundu kingdom called Ndongo. It was ruled by an *ngola* which was the title of the ruler. The Portuguese mistook the king's title for the name of the country and introduced the term Angola as a name for the whole region which came under Portuguese domination. In the same way, "Congo" refers to the historical Kingdom of Kôngo in northern Angola whose area at times extended into present-day Congo, and not to the modern state. Courtesy of Austrian National Library.

Fig. 2. "Marché aux Nègres." One of Rugendas's drawings of 1835, showing deported Africans in Rio de Janeiro after arrival. Among other important details in this "auction market," Rugendas notes how some of the young boys make drawings on the wall: the slave ship, faces with Caucasoid features (probably the sailors or slave traders), a human figure with hands stretched out as if crying for help. Rugendas wrote that the crossing from Africa to the Americas was really something like a *death* for the individual, wiping out almost completely all former ideas and interests by the excess of violent impressions. Courtesy of Austrian National Library.

Today ethnic divisions in Brazil are difficult to trace. But the former ethnic divisions live on as *cultural groupings.* Although the ethnic identity of African peoples in Brazil disintegrated gradually after 1888, when no further *ethnic reinforcements* came to Brazil from Africa, ethnic identity has been successfully transformed in Brazil into cultural identity. The cultural units are still present to a great degree among people living in the *favelas* (the Brazilian shanty-towns). Regardless of the genealogy of their members, a certain separate continuity of Nigerian and Angolan cultures, for instance, is still clearly perceptible in Brazil today, in spite of a lot of blending, many new developments and so on. Tourists are also often astonished to see white Brazilians fully participating in the *Candomblé* ritual ceremonies and religious ideas. Brazil is an instructive example for the learnability of culture.

In Brazilian history the extent of cultural exchange with Black Africa is indeed remarkable. It was a continuous process of *exchange* and not a one-way cultural impact linked to a one-way dislocation of peoples known as the slave trade. The ships went back to Africa; there were African servants on board. Later, in the nineteenth century, wealthy Brazilian Africans traded a lot with cities in Dahomey and southwestern Nigeria. African-Brazilians resettled in the area and introduced the famous Brazilian architectural style to be seen in Lagos, Ibadan, Oshogbo and other cities of Nigeria.

Ships between Angola and Portugal usually went via Brazil before Brazilian independence in 1822. In all, a situation emerged where in the periods of intensive contact with Africa it did not usually take a long time until a new dance, a new popular song or a new musical fashion coming up in Luanda or Lagos was known among the Black population of Rio de Janeiro, Salvador or Recife.

The Angolan cultural dimension in Brazil has so far been studied very little, though the Angolan presence testified by an abundance of Angolan words in the Brazilian language, *calunga* (= kalunga), *quilombo* (= kilombo), *vissungo* (= vissungo),[2] *gunga* (= ngunga) and many others, is overwhelming. Professor Fernando A. A. Mourão, Director of the Centro de Estudos Africanos of the University of São Paulo, complained

6

bitterly about the general neglect of Bantu Africa in favor of "Sudanic" West Africa in the historical study of African-Brazilian cultures.[3]

One of the reasons for the preference for West Africa, according to Mourão, was the opinion of many Brazilian and expatriate researchers of the past that West Africans, in particular the Yorùbá, had a "higher culture" than Bantu Africans. Impressed by the *orisa* pantheon, these authors felt that Angolan and Mozambiquan Africans in Brazil had hardly anything equally interesting to offer for scholarly studies. Another reason, Mourão says, was the generally distorted perception of Africa from the viewpoint of Brazil.

As elsewhere in the Americas, a panoramic view of Africa still prevails in most Brazilian writings. A further reason could have been that Angola, Brazil's main Bantu-African connection, had been for a long time a little known area culturally, with the exception of the Lunda and Chokwe group in the northeast. Angolan music, in particular, was virtually unsurveyed until the 1960s, and it is still widely unstudied until today.

For some years a research program has been going on at the Centro de Estudos Africanos in São Paulo to change this state of affairs. When I lectured there in November 1975 I met a number of active research scientists from the Angola and Congo region, among them Henriques Serrano from Cabinda and the Congolese musicologist Kazadi wa Mukuna, who kindly attended some of my lectures.

I myself worked in Angola in 1965 from July to December with financial assistance from the Junta de Investigações do Ultramar, Lisboa, on recommendation by the Late Professor Dr. António Jorge Dias and his wife, Margot Dias, of the Centro de Estudos de Antropologia Cultural. I concentrated in three areas: 1) in the Southwest (Quilengues, Dinde); 2) in the southeastern Distrito Cuando-Cubango; and 3) in eastern Angola from Vila Luso to Teixeira de Sousa and Cazombo. Subsequently, I was able to continue cultural field-work in a border area of Angola and Zambia on the Zambian side (Kabompo District) from July to December 1971 studying among Luchazi-speaking populations. This work was continued during shorter visits in 1973, 1975 and 1977.

My Brazilian field-work in October 1974 and September to November 1975 was a by-product of a lecture tour sponsored by the German Cultural Centers in Brazil with assistance from München. In 1974 I visited Salvador/Bahia in the company of a renowned musician from Malawi, Donald Kachamba, whose southeast African cultural background helped us to single out what could possibly be Mozambiquan traits. His most impressing finding was not in the field of music, however. He was able to establish a convincing identity between the distilled alcohol called *cachaça* in Brazil and the stuff known in Malawi and northern Mozambique as *kachasu*.[4] The term *cachaça* had long been on the list of African-Brazilian words of "unknown origin" in the Brazilian socio-ethnographic literature.

In 1975 I had an opportunity to work in Salvador and its suburbs for about four weeks, assisted in my endless foot-slogs by the Bahian percussionist Vicente dos Santos (Fig. 3). Vicente, who played in the Afro-Bahian Soul group *Os Erectos* in 1975 and is now with *Mar Revolto*, was born in a rural area of Bahia. He is a well-spring of traditional stories, riddles and other oral material and an expert on various traditional percussion instruments, including the musical bow. During my work in Salvador I was also assisted by Manoel de Almeida Cruz and Roberto Santos of the *Núcleo Cultural Afro-Brasileiro*, a local Black studies group.

Fig. 3. One of the musicians who assisted me in Salvador/Bahia: Vincento dos Santos. Photo by Gerhard Kubik, September 1975.

Herr Dieter Föhr of the Instituto Cultural Brasil-Alemanha in Salvador helped me greatly in making various contacts in 1974 and 1975. He also made it possible for me to record *Candomblé* and groups of street *Samba*.

Later in 1975 I did some comparative, mainly historical, studies in Rio de Janeiro and São Paulo. Here I was given every conceivable help by Professor Mourão, Senhora Haydee Nascimento and Professor Rossini Tavares de Lima of the Museu de Artes e Técnicas Populares, São Paulo, and students in my Seminar.

TIME-LINE PATTERNS

Anyone familiar with Brazilian street *samba,* as it can be seen at Carnival time in Rio de Janeiro or in Salvador/Bahia during the periods of little rain, might be conscious of a characteristic percussive pattern which permeates this music as a most persistent trait.[5] It can be played on various instruments, for instance on a high-pitched drum, on the rim of a drum, or even on a guitar. It is a focal element in which all the other instrumentalists, the singers and dancers find a pivot point for their orientation.

There are several such percussive guiding patterns found in African-Brazilian music. In the Yorùbá-originated *Candomblé* ceremonies of Bahia, they are usually struck on a double-bell with the Yorùbá name *agogo* of which only one tone is used.[6] It is essential that such rhythms be one-note patterns. While the *agogo* produces the guiding line, the same pattern is played together with its complementary rhythm on one of the drums of a three-drum *Candomblé* set. This drum is the *rumpi.*[7]

Kwabena Nketia calls such patterns *time-keeper* or *time-line* patterns. They project the time-line in many kinds of African music and are prominent particularly along the West African Coast and in Western Central Africa (Angola, Congo, Congo Brazzaville, some areas of Zambia, etc.). In a sense their function is analogous to the different meters in the predominantly monometric Western music, though a cross-cultural comparison of African versus European music is not necessarily productive. In one of his recent works Nketia writes:

> Because of the difficulty of keeping subjective metronomic time [...], African traditions facilitate this process by externalizing the basic pulse. As already noted, this may be shown through hand clapping or through the beats of a simple idiophone. The guideline which is related to the time span in this manner has come to be described as a *time-line*.[8]

Time-line patterns in African music have an intrinsic structure. Western authors have often described them as "additive rhythms." When conversing with African musicians in their own languages, however, as I have been able to do, for instance in Angola and northwestern Zambia, one cannot find a trace of an "additive" concept. Some time ago I wrote a basic paper on how timeline patterns are learned by African children in various societies with the aid of *mnemonic syllables* or *verbal mnemonics,* a system of transmission that can be described as oral notation.[9] In the mnemonic syllables associated with time-line patterns their inner-rhythmic structure reveals itself. The phonetics of the mnemonic syllables change slightly as one goes from one language area to another, together with variations in the conceptualizations of the rhythm patterns themselves. But there are some recurrent traits in this system valid throughout much of the vast stretch of African land where time-line patterns occur.

In West and Central Africa some specific time-line patterns are important. One is the so-called *twelve-pulse standard pattern.* It extends over twelve smallest time units or "elementary pulses." Therefore, we put the number 12, encircled, at the beginning of its notation, instead of a conventional "time sig-nature." In its *seven-stroke* version it can be found all along the West African coast, among the Igbo, Yorùbá, Fõn and Akan group of peoples as well as others. With the deportation of Yorùbá, Fõn and Ewe to Brazil and the transplantation of Yorùbá religious practices this pattern has become one of the hall-marks of *Candomblé* music.

WEST-AFRICAN TWELVE-PULSE STANDARD PATTERN

(*struck on a bell, high-pitched drum, glass bottle, etc.*)

a) *Seven-stroke version* (with Yorùbá mnemonic syllables col-lected from musicians in Duro Ladipo's theatrical group, in Oshogbo, 1963)

(12)	X .	X .	X X .	X .	X X .
	kɔŋ	kɔŋ	kɔlɔ	kɔŋ	kɔlɔ

b) *Five-stroke version*

(12)	X .	X .	X . .	X .	X . .

In its five-stroke version this pattern is reduced to its essentials, symbolized by all the *kɔ* syllables in the associated mnemonic pattern (For a full exposition of this subject, see my publi-cations elsewhere, 1969, 1972 and 1973).[10] This version is also found in West Africa. I recorded it in Nigeria in 1963 among the Yorùbá. Laz E. N. Ekwueme also reports it from the West coast of Africa.[11] It is equally present in the *Candomblés* of Brazil.[12]

However, the five-stroke version is much more important in Central Africa. In some areas, for instance among the Mpiemo of Central Africa and southeastern Cameroon, it is present to the exclusion of the seven-stroke variety.[13]

In Angola, both the seven and the five-stroke versions occur. The seven-stroke version is, however, accentuated differently from what can be heard on the West Coast. It is also differently placed against the basic steps of the dancers. At least with the large Ngangela ethnic group in the eastern half of Angola the second note of the double-strokes (see above) is struck very lightly, the beater just "snaps back" without investment of much new striking energy by the player. Also in Angola it is usually struck on the corpus of a drum (in the eastern half of the country), or it appears as a pattern for hand-clapping, for instance in Ombanda of southwestern Angola.[14] These are significant characteristics with reference to African-Brazilian studies.

The second important time-line pattern to be discussed is *sixteen* pulses long. In the eastern half of Angola this pattern and the associated dance movement are known as *kachacha*, for instance among the Luvale, Chokwe and peoples of the large Ngangela group.[15] It is also an important pattern in the music of Katanga (Shaba province), Congo. David Rycroft transcribed it in his analysis of Katangan guitar music.[16] The Congolese musicologist Kazadi wa Mukuna has also mentioned and transcribed it in his articles.[17]

(often struck on the corpus of a drum, on a glass bottle, calabash, or clapped by hands)

a) *Nine-stroke version* (with Ngangela mnemonic syllables, obtained at village of Soma Kayoko, area of Cuito-Cuana-vale, 1965)

$$
\left(16\right) \left| \begin{array}{l} \text{x .} \quad \text{x .} \quad \text{x .} \quad \text{x x .} \quad \text{x .} \quad \text{x .} \quad \text{x x .} \\ \text{ŋbɔ} \quad \text{ŋbɔ} \quad \text{ŋbɔ} \quad \text{ŋbɔlɔ} \quad \text{ŋbɔ} \quad \text{ŋbɔ} \quad \text{ŋbɔlɔ} \end{array} \right|
$$

b) *Seven-stroke version* (for instance, as a clap pattern in the *Nkili* dance of the Humbi, southwestern Angola, 1965)

$$
\left(16\right) \left| \text{x .} \quad \text{x .} \quad \text{x .} \quad \text{x . .} \quad \text{x .} \quad \text{x .} \quad \text{x . .} \right|
$$

This pattern has a characteristic geographical distribution in Black Africa. It is almost exclusively concentrated in Bantu-speaking Africa, mainly in Angola and adjacent areas of Congo and Zambia. In West Africa it is unimportant.

This is the pattern that marks the street *Samba* music of the Carnival de Rio and the beaches of Salvador/Bahia on a hot Sunday when literally hundreds of amateur or semi-professional *Samba* bands swarm out of the city to play on the beaches, in the little pubs and bars, or on the roads (Fig. 4). These groups sometimes use home-made instruments and in most cases employ various drums (*bombo, surdo,* etc.), *pandeiro* (tambourine), *chocalho* (long tube-rattle), and sometimes an iron bell (*agogo*) and friction drum (*cuica*) (Fig. 5).

Fig. 4

Fig. 5

I remember a significant statement by my musician friend Donald Kachamba during our joint visit to Salvador in 1974. Since he knew Nigeria and many other countries of Africa from our musical tours, the Yorùbá cultural heritage of the *Candomblés* we had seen was obvious. But on the next day, when we saw street *Samba* in Salvador, he burst out: "Now Nigeria is finished; we are in Angola." Indeed we had left one culture and penetrated another—in the same city.

Characteristically, the sixteen-pulse standard pattern is absent in Yorùbá *Candomblés*, as it is absent in Yorùbá music of the African homeland; and the twelve-pulse pattern is absent in *Samba*. There are two major African cultures in this city which are to a certain extent mutually exclusive: on the one side the Yorùbá and Ewe (Gêgê) ceremonial gatherings, on the other *Capoeira, Maculele, Samba* and the minority "Congo and Angola" ceremonies.

The word *Samba* is likely to be of Angolan origin, though it occurs as a verb in many Bantu languages I know and is often associated with specific types of body movement. In the large Ngangela group of dialects in inner Angola *kusamba* (v.) means to skip, gambol, expressing an overwhelming feeling of joy.[18] It is possible that Angolans in Brazil originally used this verb during the *batuques* (generic name for dances of Angolan origin) in the imperative. In moments of heightened physical and psychical states some people perhaps shouted to the solo dancer: "Samba! Samba!" (Skip! Gambol!). As time passed the word could have become a new label for the dance itself. I have no historical evidence for this, but in Bantu-Africa this is the way many names for dances or new musical styles originated. In the area of São Paulo in Brazil the terms *batuque* and *samba* are often used by rural people indiscriminately which fits well into the picture.

The Brazilian term *Samba* could also be linked with another word, *semba,* found in Kimbundu, Ngangela and other Angolan languages, and meaning pelvic movements that were often qualified as "obscene" by external observers. *Semba* also refers to a belly bounce, a dance tradition from the eastern hinterland of Luanda which lives on in Brazil under the famous name *umbigada.* When Portuguese phonetics are projected on the Kimbundu word *semba* it would easily assume the written form *samba.* Some tests I made with Bahian musician friends in 1975 have confirmed that the Brazilian nasal pronunciation of the term *samba* constitutes the most likely Portuguese phonetic adaptation of the Angolan word *semba.*

Time-line patterns are so important structurally in those types of African music based on them that we can confidently call them the metric back-bone of these musical types. They are orientation patterns, steering and holding together the motional process, with participating musicians and dancers depending on them. In this quality the removal or even slight modification of a time-line pattern immediately leads to the disintegration of the music concerned.

Consequently, time-line patterns must have been a rather stable element in African music history. Though West African music has changed considerably during the past three centuries and has produced in the last hundred years highlife, juju music and many other new types, the time-line patterns are still there. It is certain that they were not "invented" in some recent historical period. They were present in West Africa in the sixteenth century and much, much earlier.

The presence or absence of one of the African time-line patterns in African diaspora music can, therefore, be considered diagnostic for historical connections with specific African cultures. In the study of African-Brazilian (and indeed other African diaspora music) with non-historical methods it may be rewarding even to start one's investigation by first checking for their presence in the musical samples at hand.

Where the *twelve-pulse* standard pattern occurs, especially in its seven-stroke version *and* when it is played on a bell or bottle, we have an almost certain clue that we have a West African coastal tradition before us, Yorùbá, Fōn, Akan or the like. Its apparent absence in Black music of North America tells us that we would be on the wrong track trying to find the historical African roots of blues and jazz exclusively on the West African coast. An important key to the African component of U. S. music history lies in the western Sudanic savannah belt, as Paul Oliver[19] has pointed out, and as is also confirmed by recent genealogical studies such as Alex Haley's.[20] But there is also a Congo and Angola "strain" in the history of Black music in the U. S. and—contrary to what has been assumed—some Mozambiquan traits.

If the twelve-pulse standard pattern is struck on the corpus or the rim of a drum an Angolan and Congo connection is possible, especially if it is related to the dancer's main steps like this:

Time-line pattern: (12) | x . x . x . x x . x . x |
Dancers' steps: | x . . x . . x . . x . . |

The presence of the *sixteen-pulse* standard pattern is always an indication of an Angolan or Congo connection. Its nine-stroke variety points more specifically to the vast hinterland of the port of Benguela (the country of the Ngangela group of peoples) as far as Lunda and even Katanga. The seven-stroke version points to southwestern Angola, the area of the Humbi, Handa, Mwila, Chipongo, or to the proximate hinterland of Benguela.

This is only an outline of the procedure. Supposed stylistic connections need verification in each case, either through the presence of other traits (accumulation) or evidence obtained from historical records.

The presence of a time-line pattern is one of the few things in African music that can be established by ear from recordings or from a live performance with reasonable confidence in one's own auditory perception.[21] Once the initial test is completed the material can be examined for the presence of other traits that tend to behave with "historical inertia." One is certain aspects of the construction methods of musical instruments (though *not* the material, which changes easily depending on the ecology and availability), names for various parts (which often turn out to be just literal translations from African languages into Portuguese, Spanish, English or French), tuning procedures and playing techniques.

Another important area of "historical inertia" is to be found in stylistic features of dance or other movement. Motional behavior tends to be conservative in some basic aspects. Some of the findings of Alan Lomax' world-wide sampling in his choreometrics project may be useful to know,[22] as well as Alfons M. Dauer's little known article on dance style areas of Black Africa.[23] For instance, motional emphasis on the pelvis, buttocks, etc., especially pelvis thrusts or circular pelvis movements described in United States jazz dance history as "Congo grind" are always suspect of a Congo and Angola background.[24]

Musical teaching methods also tend to be stable in African musical cultures, especially the widespread use of syllabic or verbal mnemonics to teach instrumental patterns, even motional patterns in dance. *Verbalization of musical patterns* is, in fact, one of the most persistent musical concepts in Black Africa as a whole. This is perpetuated in Black Music of the Americas including the United States. In the Drum-and-Five Bands of the South basic drum patterns are verbalized (in English). The American folklorist Professor David Evans recently played some of his excellent recordings to me.[25]

Vicente dos Santos in Bahia once revealed to me what he thought when he was playing the Bahian musical bow: "Eu toco berimbau cantando lá dentro" (I play *berimbau* singing there inside!) He also made a recording with me in which he played a small *tamborin* while singing the syllabic patterns he used to memorize his drum phrases.[26]

In African traditions of the Americas one can find the following kinds of mnemonics: *syllabic patterns* (i.e., patterns without any verbal meaning) that sometimes are made up of a phonetic repertory derived from African languages and *verbal patterns* either in the locally spoken dialect of a European language or made up of fragments of African words or phrases.

A further important test is to check the relation of the time-line patterns to the dancers' main footsteps (the "beat" or gross-pulse) from watching a live performance or analyzing a film. The West African twelve-pulse standard pattern is generally conceived as a *ternary* rhythm from the point of view of the dancers' beat-representing steps (which is not necessarily the point of view of each of the participating musicians). In this case the dancers perform four or two main steps to the twelve pulses of the time-line, while other parts of the body move simultaneously in a different rhythm.

However, the pivot points may change as one goes from one West African culture to the next. There is a difference, for instance, between the Igbo and Yorùbá conceptualization of the same twelve-pulse standard pattern. In Brazilian *Candomblé* the slow left-right alternating steps of the ceremonially dressed women clearly go in the Yorùbá way to the bell, as Donald Kachamba and I observed in 1974, namely:

Agogo:	(12)	x	.	x	.	x	.	x	x	.	x	.	x
Dancers' steps:		r	.	l	r	.	.	l	.	r	l	.	.

But in Angola the twelve-pulse pattern is conceived differently: it stands in a different position to the dancers' steps.

Among five groups playing street *Samba* which I recorded together with Dieter Föhr of the Instituto Cultural Brasil-Alemanha at Itapoá (a suburb of Salvador) in October 1975, four clearly represented extensions of an Angolan tradition, while only one sounded unmistakably Yorùbá. The "Angolan" sounding groups were characterized by the presence of the seven-stroke version of the sixteen-pulse pattern, the presence of a *cuica* friction drum, and multi-part singing in parallel lines, mainly thirds, within a hexa-heptatonic tone system. The group which sounded Yorùbá was characterized by the absence of all these traits and the presence of unison singing (including octaves), a pentatonic tone system, Yorùbá-type voice production, Yorùbá-style melodic ductus and a slight tendency towards melismas.[27]

It was apparent that, in contrast to the Yorùbá tradition, the "Angolan" strain in Afro-Bahian music had easily assimilated certain elements of Western European *strophic form,* solo and refrains in the songs' structure, and diatonic harmony. The presence of modality and parallel thirds in the "Angolan" strain of street *Samba* could be easily interpreted as "Portuguese." The fact is, however, that in the domain of tone systems and multi-part singing Angolan and Portuguese traits reinforced each other in Brazil. The *near-equiheptatonic* tone system of inland Angola structurally linked with singing in (neutral) third-plus-fourth or third-plus-fifth chains and the *diatonic* tone system of Western European folk music linked with singing in major/minor parallel thirds made a perfect blend possible in Brazil.[28] Yorùbá music on the other hand continued in Bahia with its pentatonic system and absence of harmonic part singing.

It may be surprising to some that there should be a strong Angolan-derived musical tradition in places like Salvador, where Yorùbá and other West African elements have been dominant in the African-Bahian population. This presence of a significant Bantu strain may be relatively recent. It is known that there was a considerable influx of African populations from the south (Rio de Janeiro, etc.) and from the north (Pernambuco) to Bahia in the late nineteenth and early twentieth century. It is also testified by all the existing sources about Rio de Janeiro in the nineteenth century (Jean-Baptiste Debret, Johann Moritz Rugendas, Thomas Ewbank, Chamberlain and others) that the Angolan element in the population (and the Bantu element in general) was very strong in and around that city.

THE PWITA AND KWIKA FRICTION DRUMS

The Angola and Congo origin of the Brazilian friction drums known as *puita* in the state of São Paulo and *cuica* in Bahia is certain. These are the Brazilian spellings of the terms. In São Paulo it was used in the dances and festivities of the *congada*, *cururu* and, more rarely, in *jongo*. Sometimes it is called *boi* (oxen), an interesting denomination.[29] In an article by Lourdes Gonçalves Furtado of the Museu Paraense Emilio Goeldi in Belém, the presence of the friction drum is also reported from the north of Brazil, the area of Belém-Pará, in the dance called *carimbó*.[30]

This dance is practiced among a population of fishermen, in which the African element is rather negligible physically. The dance itself, however, is of "African origin" according to oral traditions collected by Furtado. The friction drum is called *onça* (the name for the Brazilian jaguar).

We can maintain with certainty that the Brazilian friction drums are of Central African and not of Iberian origin. A basic difference between the two is that the Brazilian varieties known under the names *puita, cuica, boi, onça* have *internal friction,* i.e., the friction stick is inside the drum, while Portuguese friction drums have *external friction.*[31] Friction drums with external friction are also present in South America: the Venezuelan *furruco,* as I saw it in the Barlovento region in September 1974, is an example.

The geographical distribution area of the African friction drum is distinctive. It mainly covers south Central Africa (Angola, southern Congo, western Zambia, and northern Botswana). Wieschhoff, basing his account on museum specimens collected in the late nineteenth and early twentieth century, wrote in 1933 that there are no convincing parallels of the African friction drum in other cultures of the world.[32]

The Brazilian designation *puita* is a Bantu word occurring in Angola and southern Congo. In 1965 I recorded friction drums called *pwita* (this is how we write it in Angolan languages) more than once in southwestern Angola among the Humbi and Handa group of peoples.[33] In one series of recordings it was played by a woman, Emilia Kakinda, ca. 40, who was known in the area as a famous *kimbanda* (indigenous doctor).[34] She was a stranger in the area, of the Mwila ethnic division; her home was at Lubango (Sá da Bandeira) (Figs. 6 and 7).

Fig. 6. The *Kimbanda* from Lubango (Sá da Bandeira), Senhora Emilia Kakinda, with members of her family. She was settled at Quicuco
(Kikuku), Circunscrição Quilengues/Dinde, in 1965. Photo by Gerhard Kubik, July 1965.

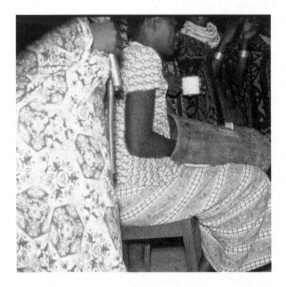

Fig. 7. Emilia Kakinda performing on the *pwita* friction drum. Girls and women in the background clap hands. Photo by Gerhard Kubik, at Quicuco (Kikuku), Circunscrição Quilengues/Dinde, southwestern Angola, July 13, 1965.

While playing she held her cylinder-shaped friction drum in her lap, the orifice directed towards her body. Next to her on the ground stood a small cup full of water. From time to time she wetted her right hand and then acted on the friction reed inside the drum, gliding along it slowly. At the same time she pressed with her left fingers from outside against the center of the drum, to alter its pitch.

The Angolan friction drums which I recorded all give a bass sound. Laurenty reported in 1972 that the Luba-Shankadi of

Katanga (southern Congo) say that a friction drum speaks with the voice of a lion.[35] Among the Luba it is called *tambwe*, meaning lion, says Laurenty. This could be compared to the Brazilian custom of giving names such as *onça* (Brazilian jaguar) or *boi* (oxen) to the African-derived varieties.

Laurenty has also contributed a useful facet about the meaning of the name *pwita*. Among the Luba-Shankadi the name occurs as a verb, *kupwita*, referring to the action of gliding along the friction stick. It means, "boire tandis que l'on émet un son par la bouche, faire du bruit avec la bouche en avalant" (to drink while a sound is emitted through the mouth, making noise with the mouth by swallowing).

In eastern Angola and northwestern Zambia the name also occurs in the Luvale language; the Luvale plural is *jipwita*. I recorded name and instrument among Lunda and Luvale musicians in the village of chief Shipwika, west of Teixeira de Sousa, in 1965.[36]

One of my Angolan friends and informants, Fortunato Pereira Gonçalves of Cuito-Cuanavale, told me in 1965 that the friction drum was also known in some parts of Angola under the name *ngoma-nkwita*. This version of the term seems to stand half-way between *pwita* and the second term found in Brazil: *cuica* (pronounced: *kwika*). My Zambian friend and co-worker Mose Yotamu, who comes from near the Angolan border, relates the Brazilian term *cuica* to East Angolan languages. In Luchazi *likwika* is a type of bird, a big bird, he says. "Wekuhandeka kwi! kwi! kwi!" (It speaks: kwi! kwi! kwi!) This is considered a bad omen (*viyovo*). A small friction drum gives exactly the same sound, says Mose.[37]

In Salvador de Bahia only the latter term, *cuica*, seems to be known, according to inquiries made for me by Dieter Föhr in 1977, while *puita* is the word known round São Paulo. Vicente dos Santos said to me in 1975: to him the syllables *pu-ita* suggested a deep tuning, while *ku-ika* suggested a high-pitched tuning. He came to this idea after hearing Angolan recordings of *pwita* I played to him. In contrast to my Angolan recordings the friction drum in all the street-bands we recorded at Itapoá "talked" with a high-pitched voice.

UMBANDA

In Angola the craft of a *Kimbanda*, such as the friction drum player Emilia Kakinda, is what is called *Umbanda* (abstract noun) in Kimbundu and related languages, or *Vumbanda* in Ngangela. The term is known in one or the other variant throughout the southern two-thirds of the territory of Angola, excluding it seems the extreme northwest (the area of the former Kingdom of Kôngo).[38]

Umbanda is the indigenous medical science of Angola. Since its concepts are based on theories about human nature which are different from those in Western cultures, *Umbanda* has often been misinterpreted by Westerners as "witchcraft." The *vimbanda* (plural of *kimbanda*) were called alternately "priests," "diviners," "witchdoctors," "prophets," "healers," "native doctors," "herbalists," etc., according to the observer's own philosophical and religious outlook.

Among the works of a *kimbanda* in Angola is, for instance, the one of making contact with a dissatisfied spirit who has afflicted a person with disease. The contact is possible through a professional medium whose body the spirit enters and through whom he speaks to the assembled audience. The audience may then ask questions to the spirit in order to find out the reasons of his dissatisfaction. I was able to document full sessions for *mahamba* (afflicting spirits) in southeastern Angola and in northwestern Zambia, when I lived in villages of the Ngangela group of peoples. This material comprising tape recordings, cinematographic shots, photographs, etc., has not yet been published.[39]

Southern Angolan medical science was exported to Brazil and is alive mainly in southern Brazil under the same name: *Umbanda*. Originally it was a purely Angolan tradition in Brazil, but gradually it came under Yorùbá cultural influence, and Yorùbá *orisa* were included into the repertory of spirits. Many Western religious and pseudo-religious elements were also incorporated even some elements of astrology.

Some Angolan keywords have persisted in Brazilian *Umbanda* until today, for instance the word *pemba* (in Angola mostly *mpemba*) for white kaolin, a substance of highly symbolic meaning in Angolan cultures; in Brazil it is used in the ceremony of *cruzamento* of a new medium and other symbolic actions.[40] The meaning of other Angolan words was forgotten in Brazil, or changed completely, for instance *kimbanda* (see above). In Brazil *quimbanda* is now the term for "bad" black magic, while *umbanda* stands for "good" white magic.[41]

White Brazilians soon perceived these practices of Black people as "spiritualism," as a "cult," even as a "religion." There is now a vast pseudo-scientific literature in Brazil about the "occultism" of *Umbandismo*, about "*magia branca*" and "*magia negra*" to be seen on the shelves of book-shops in Rio de Janeiro and São Paulo.[42]

Some of the Angolan instruments appearing in *Umbanda* sessions of southwestern Angola are also characteristic of the Brazilian extensions. In the group of Emilia Kakinda recorded in 1965 there was a tall drum (single-skin, slightly goblet-shaped, with a characteristic stand) called *kenjengo*. It is a common drum among the Humbi and Handa group of peoples in southwestern Angola. In Brazil it is not unknown.

Oneyda Alvarenga gives a photograph (fig. 33, in chapter eight) of a specimen of this type of drum, without being able, however, to identify it.[43] Another important instrument used by Emilia Kakinda's group was a rattle named *mashakashaka* (The name is ideophonic, imitating the sound of the rattle pattern *sha-ka-sha-ka*, etc). This kind of rattle has a characteristic double-cone shape with a handle. It is made from tin iron, shaping the two parts of the head like drinking cones and then soldering them together.

In Angola this kind of rattle is not only found in the southwest. I photographed it also as far east as village Sangombe, in the area of Cuito-Cuanavale, Distrito Cuando-Cubango, in 1965. It was held by a masked figure, the famous *chileya* ("the fool, jester"), which appeared in the village. Characteristically, I did not find this type of rattle used in ordinary dance music of the Ngangela and Mbwela people of this district.

Its association in Angola with a *kimbanda* on the one hand and a *likisi* (masked person) on the other may be significant. In Brazil it is an important instrument in *Umbanda*, but it is also used in the *Congada* and some other traditions with an Angola and Congo connection. The name generally reported from Brazil is *ganzá*.[44]

I did not hear this name as a term for a rattle in those areas of Angola where I worked. But it is likely that the original Angolan name was *nganza* and not *ganzá*. In the Ngangela language, for instance, *nganza* (also written *ngandza)* means a cup, a vessel, a glass for drinking.

In the collection of Latin-American instruments which the Instituto Interamericano de Etnomusicologia y Folklore (INIDEF) is building up in Caracas, there are three excellent examples of the Brazilian *ganzá*. Object No. 247 was collected by Walter Guido on March 7, 1974, in the Libreria Umbandista São Jorge, in the town of Santa Ana do Livramento, Rio Grande do Sul. It was used as "a song accompaniment in the cult of 'Umbanda.'" Two more *ganzá* that look like old instruments were collected by the young Brazilian musicologist José Jorge de Carvalho at Juazeiro Norte, on May 3, 1976.

CAPOEIRA ANGOLA

The Brazilian *Capoeira* game has attracted the attention of several cultural scientists. The most comprehensive study, so far, is by Waldeloir Rego.[45] In its present form as a stylized dance and fight game *Capoeira* originated in Brazil in the *senzulas* (the settlements of black populations on the plantations). As I see it from the viewpoint of my Angolan experience the music of *Capoeira* shows a strong Angolan heritage. The *capoeiristas* are conscious of the Angolan connection. There are many Angolan words in the songs published, for instance, by Waldeloir Rego, recognizable by someone who speaks Angolan languages. There are references to Angola in the denomination of the *toques* of *Capoeira*, i.e., the instrumental patterns for the musical bow, such as "Benguela"; and the name itself, *Capoeira Angola*, for that kind of *Capoeira* considered by its exponents as traditional, in contrast to *Capoeira Regional* (Figs. 9 and 10).

Fig. 8. *Capoeira* scene from the early 1820s in Rio de Janeiro by English painter Augustus Earle, showing two *capoeiristas* accompanied by a drummer (seated).

Fig. 9. *Capoeira* performance on the square in front of the Mercado Modelo in Salvador. Some passers-by have formed a circle and give small presents of money to the group when a round is completed. One of the *capoeiristas* is seen in the *golpe* known as *Aú*. Photo by Gerhard Kubik (F 178), Salvador/Bahia, September 20, 1975.

Fig. 10. The musicians of the *Capoeira* group play *berimbau* (gourd-resonated musical bow) with *cuxixi* (plaited rattle), *atabaque* (conical drum) and *pandeiro* (tambourine) which is not played at the moment. The members of the group are both fighters and musicians and interchange their roles. They wear a characteristic uniform: a type of "sailors' pants" with a bell bottom. Photo by Gerhard Kubik (F 179), Salvador/Bahia, September 20, 1975.

Capoeira was developed by Angolans in Brazil on the plantations of Bahia during the eighteenth and nineteenth centuries as training for possible guerilla warfare. They assembled on the plantations, often in the night, to practice various positions and techniques of attack and defense, usually without arms, but sometimes with knives: what was later to be called *golpes* in *Capoeira* terminology. The meetings were held together musically by a drum, capable of talking, and so able to direct and control the movements of the trainees.[46]

A revealing nineteenth century description, illustrated with a picture (reproduced here) is found in Johann Moritz Rugendas, 1835, under the title, "Jogar Capoëra ou danse de la guerre" (Fig. 11.) The drummer seen in the picture obviously communicates with the two opponents, by giving them orders with his talking drum. His eyes are fixed at one of the fighters. No other instruments, such as are used in present-day *Capoeira*, are drawn or mentioned by Rugendas. The accompaniment in Rugendas' time consisted of drum and hand-clapping.

Fig. 11. "*Jogar Capoeira* ou danse de la guerre" (Jogar [playing] Capoeira or war dance). An early nineteenth century illustration of *Capoeira* by Johann Moritz Rugendas, who described it as a war dance in 1835. Courtesy of Austrian National Library.

When the White owners of the plantations approached from their *casa grande*, the Blacks interrupted their training and modified it a little to look like a dance, the harmless "a brincar de Angola." Usually a signal by the drum warned the participants that a White man was approaching.[47]

This pattern of organizing resistance is very familiar from Black Africa. It could have been hardly "invented" in Brazil.

Dollar Brand, the South African pianist, described to me one kind of stylized fighting practiced in Soweto which he himself compared to *Capoeira* of Brazil.[48] Another parallel from South Africa is to be found in the origins of the *kwela* penny whistle bands: the forbidden dice gambling at street corners. When the green South African police van popularly called *kwela-kwela* approached a group of gambling youths, one of them shouted *kwela*, they pulled out their instruments and the event was transformed into a "harmless" musical performance.[49]

In Angola traditions of training for war have been reported since the earliest days of contact with the Portuguese. Cavazzi in 1687 described and depicted musical instruments used in war dances in what is now northern Angola. In 1965 I recorded in southwestern Angola, among the Humbi and Handa group, a sham stick fight for men which can possibly be related to another fictitious fighting game known in Brazil: *Maculele*.[50] Today, *Capoeira* and *Maculele* are sometimes performed in Salvador by the same groups.

In the nineteenth century Johann Moritz Rugendas reports that there was another fighting game besides *Capoeira* in which sticks were used. Unfortunately he does not report what it was called. Like *Capoeira* he calls it a "war dance" and says that two parties armed with sticks stood opposing each other, and the art was to evade the hits of the opponent.[51]

The etymology of the name *Capoeira* and its origin has not been elucidated so far with certainty. I doubt that the Portuguese word *capoeira*, meaning chicken coop, is more than a mere phonological coincidence. The origins of the Brazilian term were sought in many directions, and the possible connections offered by the authors cover pages.[52] It was thought by some that the word *capoeira* comes from Tupi and Guarani or other Amerindian languages. Strangely, hardly anyone seems to have thought of a possible African origin.

I think that *Capoeira* may well have been a *code word* by the Angolans in Brazil for their secret training. Perhaps there was really something like an "operation capoeira" in the making. In this case the Portuguese term *capoeira*, meaning chicken coop, would have been used as a symbol for something much more "classified." This was probably kept secret for a long time.

This would neither confirm nor exclude the possibility that the Brazilian word *capoeira* is Angolan. It is legitimate at least to consider this possibility. In this case we have to transcribe the word back into a Bantu orthography before undertaking further investigations: *kapwera.* The plural could have been either *vapwera* or *tupwera.*

If *capoeira* is indeed an Angolan word its coincidental pho-nemical identity with the Portuguese word meaning "chicken coop" could have been accepted by the freedom fighters with a great laugh. In this case they could speak the word into the White Man's face and enjoy the fact that he was only able to know the stupid meaning it had in his own language, unable to discover what it meant to the Angolans in Brazil.

After the abolition of slavery in 1888 the social context of *Capoeira* began to change in the new situation. What had been a systematic training for possible insurrection (and there were quite a number of insurrections besides the famous ones) now gradually became an acrobatic game.[53] But even at this stage *Capoeira* was still perceived as undesirable by the authorities. During the early twentieth century it was often prosecuted by police who appeared on horses, the *cavalaria*. From there comes the name of a famous *toque*, an instrumental pattern for the accompanying musical bow. It is called *cavalaria*. As soon as the police approached with their horses the musicians

40

changed their rhythm and played the pattern called *cavalaria* to warn all participants.

Some patterns for the accompanying musical bow called *berimbau* (pronounced: *virimbau*) can be traced back to the *mbulumbumba* gourd-resonated bow of southwestern Angola. I was very surprised to discover this when playing some of my Angolan bow recordings to Vicente dos Santos in Salvador, Lygia Carvalho and other informants in Rio de Janeiro. The African-Brazilians *understood* the music of the southwestern Angolan *mbulumbumba*. Especially my recordings of the Angolan musician José Virasanda provoked a surprising reaction.[54] Vicente in Salvador and others in Rio de Janeiro and São Paulo immediately said that the first pattern played by Virasanda was called *São Bento Grande* in *Capoeira;* and the second rhythm which he *suddenly* introduces without stopping his play was called *Cavalaria.*

It is not exactly known when the Brazilian gourd-resonated bow was integrated into *Capoeira*. Rugendas in 1835 does not mention it, and his picture only shows a drum. From other historical illustrations of the early nineteenth century, particularly the pictures of Jean-Baptiste Debret (fig. 12) and Lieutnant Chamberlain (fig. 13), it is evident that the gourd-resonated musical bow was popular as a *solo* instrument at that time in Rio de Janeiro.[55] Debret in the notes to his pictures gives the name *oricongo*,[56] while Chamberlain mentions *madimba lungungo*.[57] Variants of these names are found in the northern third of Angola and in southern Congo among the Holo, Mbala, Sonde, Luluwa and others.[58]

Fig. 12. Debret's illustration, "Le vieil Orphée africain 'Oricongo'" (The old African Orpheus 'Oricongo'). In his explanatory notes he says the following (in English translation): "This instrument consists of a half of a gourd adhering to a bow formed by a curved rod with a brass wire pulled tight, which is struck slightly. One can, at the same time, study the musical instinct of the player, which supports a hand calabash on his or her uncovered belly, for at the same time, by vibration, a more serious and more harmonious sound; [... He or she] gets it by tapping gently on the rope with a small stick held between the index and the medium of the right hand. The drawing shows the misfortune of an old enslaved African reduced to beggary." Courtesy of Fundação Raymundo Otloni de Castro Maya, Rio de Janeiro.

Fig. 13. Lieutenant Chamberlain's illustration, "A market stall." From his 1822 description, Chamberlain wrote, "The Negro with a loaded basket on his head, though arrested in his progress by what is going on, does not however cease playing upon his favorite *madimba lungungo,* an African musical instrument in the shape of a bow, with a wire instead of a string. At the end where the bow is held is fixed an empty calabash or wooden bowl, which being placed against the naked stomach enables the performer to feel as well as to hear the music he is making. The manner of playing is very simple. The wire being well stretched, is gently struck, producing a note which is modulated by the fingers of the other hand pinching the wire in various places according to the fancy; its compass is very small and the airs played upon it are few; they are generally accompanied by the performer with the voice and consist of ditties of his native country sung in his native language." Courtesy of Biblioteca Nacional, Rio de Janeiro.

It appears that the musical bow was integrated into *Capoeira* about the same time when it changed to become an "acrobatic wrestling dance game"; that was at the turn of the century. *Why* the instrumental basis changed, and *why* the musical background in modern *Capoeira* is now composed of two to three musical bows, *pandeiro* and sometimes *atabaque* (drum) is something one may speculate about. It seems to coincide historically with the influx of non-Yorùbá Black people from southern Brazil to Salvador/Bahia. The increasing contacts between Bantu and non-Bantu Africans in Brazil created the possibility of an effective blending of several African traditions.

Such blending was easy in those traits where the African traditions showed similarities or analogies that could be re-interpreted. In this context it may be worth pointing out that traditions to accompany fighting games with musical instruments are not restricted at all to Angola and southern Africa. The Nigerian socio-linguist Valentine Ojo told me in June 1977, when we met during the Jazz Congress in Graz, that the large Yorùbá lamellophone called *agidigbo* (which is almost exactly like the Cuban *marimbula*) was used long ago as an instrument to accompany a wrestling game called *gidigbo*. So there is a Yorùbá tradition of accompanying wrestling games with "melodic" instruments.

It is quite possible that Yorùbá concepts about the musical background of wrestling games slipped into *Capoeira* at a stage when it began to lose its older social context, and, as a consequence, was dangerously exposed to the possibility of disappearing. I have not found any trace of the Yorùbá *agidigbo* in Brazil, and I am not suggesting that the Yorùbá wrestling game was exported there and merged with the older *Capoeira*. Culture is not necessarily exported in its visually and auditively perceptible dimension only. There was a *readiness* in Yorùbá culture to use melodic instruments for the accompaniment of such games. ✗

Projected on *Capoeira*, the Yorùbá concept would have stimulated the use of more and other instruments besides the traditional drum. At the same time the Angolan carriers of the *Capoeira* tradition would have resisted too many compromising changes which could have led to the disappearance of the Angolan identity of this tradition. The compromise solution resulting from cultural pressure of the other African group and intra-cultural resistance of the Angolans would have been that the carriers of *Capoeira* were willing to include more instruments, but preferred to adopt an instrument *which was also Angolan:* the gourd-resonated musical bow. This might be the story of how the gourd bow, in Angola and Brazil of past centuries a *solo* instrument, became a group instrument in Brazilian *Capoeira*.

Recently, *Capoeira* has begun to change again in Salvador/ Bahia under the influence of a newly imported tradition of acrobatic fighting with a number of meeting points and similarities with *Capoeira*: *kung-fu* and *karate*. The young *capoeiristas* in Salvador love to see the "Eastern" movies imported from Hong Kong starring Bruce Lee and other famous fighters. In 1975 Vicente dos Santos and I watched a performance of *Capoeira* in the Teatro Castro Alves, Salvador, where some "beats" (*golpes*) from *kung-fu* were beautifully integrated into the graceful movement repertoire of the *capoeiristas*.

THE BERIMBAU MUSICAL BOW

A Brazilian *berimbau de barriga* can be bought in the big cities, especially in Salvador.[59] The specimens sold to tourists in the Mercado Modelo of Salvador are not the best instruments, however, for playing. Vicente dos Santos, who had been a player of the *berimbau* as a young boy, was not happy with the one we bought there for our own use in October 1975. The calabash, though nicely painted, was too small, and not in tune with the string, he explained. After long excursions on foot through the *favelas* we were able to meet the right people so that Vicente could procure himself a large and beautiful calabash (Figs. 14 and 15).

Fig. 14. The *berimbau* restored by Vincente dos Santos with its large calabash and the *caxixi*. Photo by Gerhard Kubik, Salvador/Bahia, October 1975.

Fig.15. Vicente dos Santos playing his *berimbau*. Clearly visible is the finger-set and the *caxixi* rattle in the right hand holding the stick. Photo by Gerhard Kubik, Salvador/Bahia, September 1975.

For the construction of a *berimbau*, said Vicente, one first needed a good branch from a tree to make the string-bearer (the bow). In his home area, some 50 km from the city of Salvador, it was usually taken from the tree named *gobiraba*, sometimes from *canela de viado*, because these woods were strong enough.

The string is made from steel wire (*arame de aço*). It is fixed to the two ends of the bow following a different system on each side. A loop is then used to attach the large calabash, dividing the string into two sections. The relation between the two parts should be 4:1, so that the shorter section sounds two octaves higher than the longer one. The shorter section's function is to give sympathetic resonance; it is not played upon except in demonstrations of all the sounds inherent in the *berimbau*. The percussionist Nana from Recife, who often performed with jazz musician Don Cherry, is a master in these techniques.[60]

The corporal pitch of the calabash should be in unison with the string. To tune it the musician cuts off carefully some material from the orifice. For playing the musician holds the *berimbau* vertically, the shorter section of the string below. In his right hand he holds his percussion stick together with a small plaited rattle called *caxixi* (pronounced: *kashishi*). The left hand holds the bow with a characteristic finger set: the second and third fingers hold the bow (string-bearer) while the fourth finger is hooked at the tuning *noose*. Between thumb and first finger he holds a so-called *dobrão*. This is the name of an old copper coin, now applied for any kind of coin (Fig. 16).

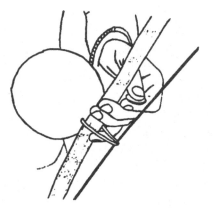

Fig. 16. The characteristic finger-set in the playing technique of the *berimbau*. Thumb and index finger of the left hand hold the *dobrão*, the little finger is hooked at the tuning-noose. Demonstrator: Vincente dos Santos. Enlarged detail copied from projected colour slide by transparency drawing method. Drawing and photo by Gerhard Kubik, Salvador/Bahia, October 1975.

When playing he strikes the longer section of the string. For obtaining the second note, which is generally about a whole-tone higher, he stops the string with the *dobrão*. A further technique is important with the *berimbau de barriga*: while playing the musician constantly changes the distance between the calabash and his abdomen (from which he has removed the shirt) to alter the sound spectrum by reinforcing certain harmonics. In this way he creates timbre sequences.

The name *berimbau* was not originally associated with the African musical bows in Brazil. In Portugal it refers to the *guimbarde* ("Jew's harp"). However, it does not sound like a Portuguese word either. This was confirmed in a conversation I had a few years ago with Professor Jorge and Margot Dias. In Brazil this word was projected on the African bows which were first known there under Angolan names. White Brazilians noticed a similarity between the guimbarde of their own cultures and the African bows in that all these instruments create melodies by reinforcing harmonics. Consequently, the African mouth-bow was easily classified as a kind of guimbarde (*berimbau de boca*); and the gourd-bow was labeled as "guimbarde of the belly" (*berimbau de barriga*). This is a familiar pattern of re-interpretation, the same that made colonial Europeans in Black Africa call the African lamellophones "hand-pianos," "thumb-pianos," "Caffir pianos" and the like.

Eventually the name *berimbau* was adopted by the African-Brazilians themselves at the expense of the original Angolan names. It was a result of the same processes of "emancipation" which turned *Capoeira* from a prosecuted activity into a harmless manifestation within a presentable White category: *Folklore.*

One of the likely areas of origin of what became the Brazilian gourd-bow is to be found in the eastern and southeastern hinterland of the port of Benguela. Organological traits of several related braced gourd-bows from Angola and southern Congo were probably merged in Brazil to form the *berimbau de barriga* as we know it today. In southwestern Angola, I recorded gourd-bows in 1965 which were called *mbulumbumba* (Fig. 17).[61] These instruments are virtually identical with the Brazilian *berimbau*. Southwest Angola was one of the main areas from where enslaved Africans were shipped to Brazil, mainly to Rio de Janeiro and Pernambuco, and to Cuba. According to oral traditions I collected in 1965 among people speaking Humbi, Handa, Chipongo, Kirenge and Mwila, the whole area east and north of Lubango (Sá da Bandeira) was literally devastated and depopulated by transatlantic slaving in periods I have estimated to be in the eighteenth century.

Fig. 17. The southwest Angolan *mbulumbumba* played by musician Chapinga, of the Chipongo ethnic division. Photo by Gerhard Kubik, at Munengole village, near the administrative post of Dinde, north of Lubango (Sá da Bandeira), July 15, 1965.

The name *mbulumbumba* was exported to Cuba together with the gourd-resonated bow. It is reported by Fernando Ortiz in 1955 under the hispanisized spelling *"burumbumba."*[62] As to

Brazil Waldeloir Rego quotes some sources mentioning the term *bucumbumba* (pronounced: *bukumbumba*) as one of the names besides *rucungo*.[63] An inventory of some 15 African names for the bow occurring in Brazil and reported in the literature shows that all were Congo and Angolan except *gubo* which occurs in *nineteenth* and twentieth century Mozambique and Malawi among the immigrating Ngoni and people who came under their influence.[64] But *gubo* is a different type of gourd-bow, it is *un*-braced. However, it is held vertically during performance.

The Brazilian gourd-bow and the southwest Angolan variety called *mbulumbumba* are identical in the construction and the playing technique, as well as in the tuning and in a number of basic patterns played. The mode of attachment of the calabash, the division of the string 4:1, and most significantly, how the player *holds* it with his left hand are all identical.[65] Though the Angolan players whom I recorded held their instruments obliquely and not vertically like the Brazilians, this is a less significant trait, as it can easily change. There are gourd-bow players, for instance among the Wasangu of Tanzania, who hold their instrument vertically in a manner so suggestive of the *berimbau* that one can easily be deceived, and yet it is a different instrument.[66]

More important is the finger-set (Figs. 18 and 19). I have not seen it anywhere else so far besides in Angola. There was only a minor difference: the Angolans stopped the string with the nail of the thumb in a kind of pincer movement of thumb and index finger, while the Brazilians had adopted a coin instead.

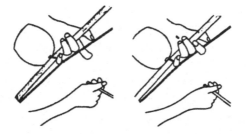

Fig.. 18 and 19 — Chapinga's finger technique: the bow lies in the palm, held by the middle and ring fingers. The little finger is hooked round the tuning-noose, pulling it a little to the left. Fig.re 18 shows the "open" position of the string, whereas figure 19 shows the stopping of the string by the thumb and index finger. The index finger stops the string with a hooking movement. The inside of the second joint pulls the string towards the bow and the string is thus pressed towards the outstretched tip of the thumb, which stops the string with the nail and thus raises the pitch. Fig.re 18 was copied from color slide F 105, figure 19 from cine film X2, by Gerhard Kubik, Munengole (southwestern Angola), July 15, 1965.

There is one significant addition to the gourd-bow in Brazil: the rattle called *caxixi*. In some way its presence is a riddle. In Angola I did not see musical bow players holding a rattle at the same time. Historical illustrations of the gourd-bow in Brazil of the nineteenth century also show no trace of a *caxixi*.

The name sounds Bantu: *kashishi*. If we take the syllables of the stem to be ideophonic, imitating the sound of a rattle *shi-shi- shi-,* and the *ka-* as a diminutive prefix, the meaning of the word *caxixi* (pronounced: *kashishi*) could be literally translated as "the small thing which *continuously* gives the sound shi-shi-," a very accurate description of the *caxixi* in musical terms. Though the name could be Angolan, or alternatively might have been created by Angolans in Brazil, the instrument itself seems to show little connection with the Angola and Congo area.

Is the *caxixi* a later addition to the Angolan gourd-bow in Brazil? Was it adopted at the time when the Brazilian gourd-bow became an *ensemble* instrument for the *Capoeira* game? Obviously, *Capoeira* is a much more noisy enterprise than the lonely self-delectative playing of the gourd-bow by a blind musician in Rio de Janeiro as depicted in one of Debret's paintings. More than one musical bow is needed in *Capoeira* to control the game. And there must be something to mark the beat of the music. In many African traditions rattles are the most important beat-carrying instruments. So it is apparent why the *caxixi* could have been integrated into the playing techniques of the bow.

But where does it come from? Without doubt it is an African instrument, but from which African tradition? From my knowledge of West and Central Africa it appears that plaited vessel rattles, bell-shaped, with a bow-grip and a base cut from a piece of gourd (turned inside out) are found especially in the eastern half of Nigeria, in a large area overlapping into northern and western Cameroon. In 1963 I recorded a horn-band in a lonely place called Kontcha on the northern Nigeria and Cameroon border. Six men of the Kutin people performed a circular funeral dance and played on end-blown composite gourd-horns. While each man held the horn with his left he shook a plaited rattle very similar to the *caxixi* with his right hand.[67]

Some of the plaited rattles from the Nigeria and Cameroon border area in possession of the Museum für Völkerkunde, Vienna, also have a base cut from a piece of calabash.[68] They are very similar to the *caxixi*. Certainly, plaited rattles made from various fiber materials have been found in *many* areas of West and Central Africa. The king's wives of Abomey (in the former Fõn kingdom of Dahomey) employ a large type, as can be seen in a film published by the Institut für den Wissenschaftlichen Film, Göttingen.[69] But the closest present-day parallels to the Brazilian *caxixi* I have seen seem to occur in the region mentioned: the eastern half of Nigeria, overlapping into western Cameroon.

In northern Angola and across the border in southwestern Congo another large type of plaited rattle is found (different from the *caxixi)* which was also exported to Brazil as part of transatlantic slaving and is known in São Paulo under the name *angoia.*[70]

THE MARIMBA OF SÃO PAULO

Marimba or *malimba* is a term found in several Bantu languages in East, Southeast and Central Africa, meaning: xylophone and/or lamellophone. In writings of the past the term was often applied incorrectly to mean African or Latin-American xylophones in general, especially referring to the gourd-resonated varieties. Lamellophones on the other hand were called *sanza*. Two "scientific" categories were thus created, *marimba* (African xylophone) and *sanza* (African lamellophone), whose semantic fields in no way correspond with comparable meanings in African languages.

Rimba (or *limba*), the word stem and singular form, means a note, a sounding key, slat or lamella. With a cumulative prefix *ma-*, it means the notes, slats, lamellae, etc., hence the complete "keyboard," the complete instrument. Among the Mang'anja and the Lomwe of Mozambique and Malawi there are one-note gourd-resonated xylophones, played in groups. Consequently one such instrument is called *limba*.[71]

The stem and prefix of this Bantu term vary somewhat as one goes from area to area, according to the phonemic repertoire of the various languages. Among Sena populations in the lower Zambezi valley xylophones are called *ulimba* or *valimba*; they are called *silimba* among the Lozi of Zambia and *jinjimba* (pronounced: ʒinʒimba) among the Luvale of Zambia and eastern Angola. Lamellophones appear as *malimba* or *ma-*

rimba in wide areas of Tanzania and as *kalimba* and *chirimba* (two types of different size) in northern Malawi.[72]

The lamellophone is often conceived as a relative of the xylophone by Bantu musicians. It is like a "small portable xylophone."[73] Therefore, people in Zanzibar call their box-resonated xylophones *marimba* and their lamellophones *marimba madogo* ("small *marimba*") to distinguish the two.[74]

With the deportation of Bantu-speaking peoples from Mozambique and Angola and Congo to the Americas the term *marimba* was also exported. In the Americas it is now usually associated with xylophones only, but there are testimonies, such as by Alexandre Rodrigues Ferreira, in 1783, that this name was also applied to lamellophones in the north of Brazil (see the next chapter) and by George W. Cable, in 1886, in New Orleans referring to a *marimba brett*.[75]

As African languages began to be forgotten in Latin America the original meaning of the word *marimba* also gradually disappeared from memory (Fig. 20). For Colombia George List reported in 1966 the application of the name *marimba* "as a generic name for all melodic non-aerophones," and in particular for the mouth-bow.[76] Obviously at this stage the semantic field of this word had widened to include a string instrument, something inconceivable from the Bantu-African point of view. The word was also modified under the impact of Spanish or Portuguese in Latin America. For instance, by the addition of the Spanish suffix *-ula* the word *marimba* became *marimbula* in Cuba, meaning a lamellophone.

Fig. 20. A *marimba* being played by captive or acculturated Africans in late eighteenth century Peru. Reproduced from Martinez Companon y Bujanda, *Trujillo de Peru* (Madrid: Ediciones Cultura Hispanica, 1978-1994), 2: plate E142.

Gourd-resonated portable xylophones are found in southern Brazil, mainly in the state of São Paulo. This is not surprising because the south of Brazil is where the Bantu population was particularly concentrated. There are several references to xylophones in Brazil. Araújo mentions two types in his *Cultura popular brasileira*, in 1973, and depicts a gourd-resonated variety with six relatively flat and broad keys, and a box-resonated variety with eleven notes on page 136; the latter resembles instruments found on the East African Coast (from the Kenyan Coast down to Tanzania), except in that it also has a rail and a string for carrying.

Rossini Tavares de Lima did some research on the *marimba* in the state of São Paulo in 1944. He published two excellent photographs of a performance he saw at Ilhabela. It was played together with drums named *tambaque* and *tambu* (Brazilian spellings) that are obviously of Congo origin.[77]

Most recently Kilza Setti, who works in the Departamento de Ciências Sociais of the University of São Paulo, did a study of *marimba* xylophones in this area. During a Seminar on African cultures I gave at the Centro de Estudos Africanos of the same University in November 1975 she presented her material as a Seminar work. Kilza Setti found portable gourd-resonated xylophones called *marimba* at Bairro de S. Francisco, Município de São Sebastião (state of São Paulo), in 1972.

The instruments she describes were played during the festivities of the *Congada*, during ceremonies in which the indigenous black population used to elect a King of Congo. There are some revealing historical descriptions by Henry Koster and by Rugendas (early nineteenth century) of the election of a King of Congo in southern Brazil.[78] Among the Congo people settled in southern Brazil some aspects of their ancient political organization were perpetuated for a long time, to the degree that a kind of fictitious Kingdom of Kôngo was established on Brazilian soil. It did not have political power and was an internal symbolic tradition among the Congo and Angola group in Brazil. The Whites usually ridiculed these ceremonies, an attitude the Africans gradually internalized themselves. As a result what had been meant originally as a serious continuation of the political heritage of the famous Kingdom of Kôngo soon became a mere farce with a lot of theatrical entertainment from various sources in it.

Kilza Setti's informants claimed that the specimens she photographed were made in the "time of the slaves". The instrument depicted in one of her photographs has ten keys and eight gourd-resonators, painted in color. It has a characteristic rail to make it portable and keep the keyboard away from the player's body. A leather string serves to hang it round the musician's shoulders. Obviously it was played *walking* or *standing*.

When I saw Setti's photographs I was struck by the similarity of the São Paulo xylophones with some I had recorded in southern Cameroon in 1960, 1964 and 1969-1970.[79] There is an oral tradition among people in southern Cameroon saying that usually four such instruments were played together during a procession. These were chiefs' instruments, and when the chief travelled the xylophone band usually went ahead walking, announcing his arrival all the way he travelled.[80]

Portable xylophones of the manufacture and shape of Setti's instruments are quite different from the large (standing) xylophones, reported, for instance, from Colombia and Ecuador which could be related to those found in the lower Zambezi valley, Mozambique, according to my evaluation. Setti's type was reported in the seventeenth century from the Kingdom of Kôngo and adjacent areas by several authors, in particular by Cavazzi in 1687 (Fig. 21).[81]

A beautiful illustration is found in Girolamo Merolla's work of 1692 from the same area (Fig. 22).[82] In Merolla's etching the name *marimba* is written below the instrument seen in the center (See reproduction). Several other Congo instruments of the time are also shown and their names given. Merolla's text reads as follows (quoted from Hirschberg's translation from Italian):

One of the most common instruments is the *marimba*. Sixteen calabashes act as resonators and are supported lengthwise by two bars. Above the calabashes little boards of red wood, somewhat longer than a span, are placed, called *taculla*. The instrument is hung round the neck [...] Mostly four marimbas are played together; if six want to play the *cassuto* is added—a hollowed piece of wood four spans long, with ridges in it. The bass of this orchestra is the *quilondo*, a roomy, big-bellied instrument two and a half to three spans in height which looks like a bottle towards the end and is rubbed in the same way as the *cassuto* [...][83]

Fig. 21. Drawings of musical instruments, including a *marimba* (center) and what looks like a *berimbau* (right), by Capuchin missionary Antonio Cavazzi, who lived in the Kingdom of Kongo in the 1670s. Reproduced from Ezio Bassani, ed., *Un Cappuccino nell'Africa nera del seicento: I disegni dei Manoscritti Araldi del Padre Giovanni Antonio Cavazzi da Montecuccolo* (Milan: Quaderni Poro, no. 4, 1987), plate 19.

Fig. 22. Girolamo Merolla's illustration of musical instruments and their players in the Kingdom of Kôngo (1692). Reproduced from Waiter Hirschberg's *Monumenta Ethnographica: Black Africa*, vol. 1. Graz, 1962.

From Brazil there is a picture of a performance in the dance *ba-ducca* (usually written *batuque)* from the area of São Paulo to be found in Martius and Spix' *Atlas zur Reise in Brasilien,* 1817-1820.[84] The picture (fig. 23) shows an excited group of dancers, men and women, and a police-man in the background watching the scene. The movements of the dancers seem to concentrate on arms, breast and hips with inflexed attitude of the legs (the typical "collapse" in Helmut Günther's terminology).[85] No jumps seem to occur and movement seems to be restricted in space. The picture strongly suggests a Congo and Angola style. In the background there is a xylophone of the type described by de Lima, Araújo, Setti and other Brazilian authors. It is accompanied with a scraper resembling the *cassuto* in Merolla's illustration from Congo.

DIE BADUCCA, IN S. PAULO

Fig. 23. "Die Baducca in S. Paulo" (The "Baducaa" dance in São Paulo), in C. F. von Martius and J. B. von Spix, *Atlas zur Reise in Brasilien* (1817-1820). The couples are doing what some have suggested is the *lundu* dance, with accompanying instruments. Courtesy of the Biblioteca Nacional, Secçào de Iconografia.

Though there is 130 years time difference between Merolla's illustration from the Kingdom of Kôngo and this document from southern Brazil, continuity in the instrumental field is clear. This continuity extends into the present time. In the former territory of the Kingdom of Kôngo itself, however circumstances have changed considerably since the end of the seventeenth century (the epoch of Cavazzi, Merolla and others). With the breakdown of the old political structure and the eventual partition of the area between Portuguese and Belgians, many musical instruments which were once associated with kingship or chieftainship have either disappeared or changed their original social context.

The portable xylophone was a representation instrument of kings and chiefs. This custom quickly spread into wide areas of western Central Africa. The organized states existing in northern Angola in the fifteenth, sixteenth and seventeenth centuries had a powerful radiation culturally and politically on neighboring areas. The *marimba* representation music swept into the interior of what is now Congo-Brazzaville. The presence of a band of portable xylophones became a symbol of authority among many of the small chieftainships north of the powerful Kingdom of Kôngo.

The xylophones described by Cavazzi and Merolla thus live on until today at the periphery of the old Kingdom of Kôngo and beyond. As recently as 1966 I found them along the Sangha river upwards (for instance among the Mpiem, who themselves migrated into their present area from the south), together with other chiefs' instruments such as large double bells (among the Pomo and Mpiemo).[86] Though the name *marimba* was not usually adopted further north, what has remained basically identical is the social context, some aspects in the construction of the instruments, and their playing techniques.

Since the sixteenth and seventeenth centuries the portable gourd-resonated *marimba* of the Kingdom of Kôngo seems to have spread out mainly in two directions: to the north with the powerful cultural radiation of the Kingdom of Kôngo; and to southern Brazil, and possibly also other areas of Latin America, for instance Nicaragua, with the deportation of people from the Kingdom of Kôngo and neighboring states.

We are referring here to a specific type of xylophone, the variety described by Cavazzi and Merolla which has survived in the places indicated. There are other types found in Congo and Angola, for example the bow-shaped, gourd-resonated variety of the Chokwe. These have another history. Regarding Latin-American xylophones in general, it is important to keep in mind that different types from different African areas are present on the American soil under the name *marimba*. The São Paulo *marimba* is one specific type, not to be confounded with the Guatemalan and Colombian instruments under the same name.

SOME EIGHTEENTH AND
NINETEENTH-CENTURY BRAZILIAN SOURCES
COMPARED WITH ANGOLAN FIELD MATERIAL

A most valuable source for African-Brazilian historical studies is Alexandre Rodrigues Ferreira's *Viagem filosófica pelas Capitanias do Grão Pará, Rio Negro, Mato Grosso e Cuiabá, 1783-1792*, published in Rio de Janeiro between 1971 and 1974. Ferreira and his assistants were experts in technical drawing. His sense for detail and accuracy in his illustrations of ships, for instance, has fascinated historians.

Ferreira was born in Bahia on April 27, 1756. He began a clerical career, later studied in Portugal and obtained a doctorate from the University of Coimbra in 1779. Until 1783 he Worked in the Real Museu d'Ajuda and also became a corresponding member of the Real Academia das Sciencias de Lisboa in 1780.

In September 1783 he set out on his famous *Philosophical Journey* at Belém/Pará in the north of Brazil, reaching Vila Bela, the capital of Mato Grosso, in 1789. He only returned in 1792 to Belém and in the following year to Portugal.[87]

Ferreira travelled in northern Brazil from Belém south and southwest in the vast forest regions and dry savannah parts. While on the coast he had contact with the African component of the population and made drawings of African instruments in great detail. It was possible for me to identify them with certainty as *Angolan-originated*.

The first drawing to be discussed shows a lamellophone described by Ferreira as "Marimba, Instrumento q̲ uzão os Prétos" (Marimba, an instrument that the Blacks use). It is characterized by the following organological traits, as can be seen in the picture (fig. 24):

1. A board-shaped corpus, almost square, made of wood.
2. A circular hole in the center of the corpus.
3. Reliefs carved (or burnt) in, mainly on the underside.
4. Sound-board and back-rest for the lamellae constitute a single piece of wood.
5. The metal bridge has a characteristic flat U-shape and is about 1.8 cm high in its central part. The ends are less high, only about 1.5 cm, which is a little higher than the back-rest.
6. There are sixteen iron lamellae.
7. They are spatula-shaped (broader at the playing ends).
8. A straining bar of iron is holding them down; it is "sewn" to the wooden board with wire running through ten little holes stitched into the board. These points are placed such that they sometimes embrace two lamellae in an order that looks regular: 1+2+2+1 for the outer lamellae of both the left and the right thumb playing areas, and 2 + 2 for the four innermost lamellae.
9. The layout of the lamellae is in a regular, flat V-form, with the deepest note in the middle.
10. Fine tuning is done by attaching black wax to the underside of the lamellae. This is why the layout is so regular.

11. The player uses his thumbs for pressing the lamellae downwards and releasing them.

12. At the edge of the board directed towards the player's chest an iron bar is attached, carrying four rattle-rings. These buzzers are meant to modify and prolong the sound by sympathetic vibration.

13. The string attached at the top of the board is for carrying the instrument.

14. This lamellophone must have been held into a calabash during performance, because it has a board-shaped corpus and no resonator of its own.

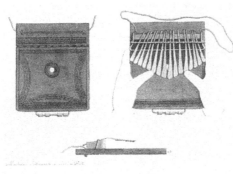

Fig. 24. "Marimba, Instrumento q. uzão os Prétos" (Marimba, an instrument that the Blacks use). Drawing of a lamellophone with distinctly Angolan characteristics found in northern Brazil in the late eighteenth century. Reproduced from Alexandre Rodrigues Ferreira's *Viagem Filosófica...* (1783-1792). Courtesy of the Biblioteca Nacional, Rio de Janeiro.

In Angola, as I know from my earlier research, this type of lamellophone is almost universally present, except in small areas of the extreme northwest. It is known as *kisanji* (including variant pronunciations such as *chisanji, chisaji, chisandzi*), which is a generic term referring to all kinds of lamellophone. The plural is *visanji*. In southwestern Angola I recorded a specimen with 16 keys in the area of Dinde/Quilengues.[88] In the vast Ngangela-speaking eastern region I saw, recorded, photographed and filmed small varieties with only lo notes reflecting in detail Ferreira's drawing from eighteenth century Brazil, except in the number of the lamellae. These instruments are called *chisanzi cha ndingo* among the Ngangela and Mbwela of the Kwitu river area, and the *chisandzi cha kakalendende* among the Luchazi groups now settled across the border in northwestern Zambia.[89] An eminent player I recorded there in 1971 was Kaunda Sakapandulula, born in 1904, just two years before his death (Figs. 25 and 26).[90]

Fig. 25. Playing techniques of Angolan board-lamellophones: *Chisandzi cha kakelendende* played by an old man, Kaunda Sakapandulula. The musician is holding his instrument into a large calabash

for added resonance. Photo by Gerhard Kubik, October 20, 1971, at Chief Kalunga's village, Chikenge, Kabompo District, Northwestern Province, Zambia.

Fig. 26. Kaunda Sakapandulula (1904 – April 20, 1973) was an eminent Luchazi player of the *chisandzi cha kakelendende*. He travelled

widely in eastern Angola reaching Lungevungu, Luchazi, Kanazi, Kwitu, Kwanavale, Kuvangu and Kwewe rivers, as far as Viye (Bié), the country of the Ovimbundu. Photo by Gerhard Kubik, October 20, 1971, at Chief Kalunga's village, Cikenge, Kabompo District, Northwestern Province, Zambia.

Margot Dias, of the Centro de Estudos de Antropologia Cultural, in Lisbon, has been kind enough to look for me through the Lisbon collection of Angolan instruments; she found several specimens from central and southwestern Angola of the same type as Ferreira's and with 16 notes. Two instruments in the Lisbon collection, she writes, are identical with Ferreira's instrument: No. AH 430 collected by Dr. Carreira in 1966 in the Serra Baixo (southwestern Angola) and No. AP 824 collected by Ernesto Veiga de Oliveira in 1971 from the Kwisi (Cuissi) near Moçâmedes.[91] In October 1977 I had the opportunity to visit Lisbon on invitation of the Museu de Etnologia and photographed one of these instruments (Figs. 27, 28 and 29).

CXLIV   *Marimba de Cafri*

Fig.. 27, 28 and 29. African lamellophones with board-shaped corpus and 8 to 10 lamellae. The first is a late seventeenth or early eighteenth century illustration of a southeast African lamellophone by Filippo

Bonanni. The other two figures are illustrations of Angolan lamellophones, some of which found their way to São Paulo and other parts
of Brazil.

There is an abundance of written and pictorial material from
nineteenth century Brazil about African-Brazilian lamellophones which are obviously of Angolan descent. Jean-Baptiste
Debret, the French painter who worked in Brazil between
1816 and 1832, depicted lamellophones played by musicians in
and around Rio de Janeiro several times (Fig. 30.) As in Angola these were played by musicians holding the board into
a large calabash, walking along with it, for instance during a
Sunday promenade in the city of Rio, or during the transpor-
tation of coffee from the interior. Thomas Ewbank describes
lamellophones with "from ten to fifteen" notes, struck with the
thumbs.[92] He writes about "[...] a slave walking along with a
load in his head and both hands in a large gourd, out of which
he drew a fashionable waltzing tune."

Fig. 30. "Marimba—La promenade du dimanche après-midi" (Marimba, public walk for a social event on a Sunday afternoon). This is one of the paintings by Jean-Baptiste Debret, who lived in Rio de Janeiro from 1816 to 1832. A group of African-Brazilians is seen in the clothing style of the Napoleonic era walking through a street of Rio de Janeiro. Two of them play lamellophones, one is clapping hands, and another is a scraper. The lamellophone player uses the thumbs; one of them is holding his instrument in a large calabash. Though they are dressed in fanciful clothes, a tradition which has survived in today's carnival, none of them has shoes on. Obviously the painter wanted to express the fact that these musicians were enslaved Africans or servants. One of them carries a flag indicating a feeling of group identity. Courtesy of Fundação Raymundò Ottoni de Castro Maya, Rio de Janeiro.

In the notes to his paintings Jean-Baptiste Debret informs us in no uncertain terms from which part of Africa the most musical portion of the population of Rio de Janeiro had come: "[...] les nègres *Bengueles* et *Angolais* doivent être cités comme les plus musiciens, et sont surtout remarquables par l'industrieuse fabrication de leurs instruments, tels que le *marimba,* la *viole d'Angola,* espèce de lyre à quatre cordes; le *violon,* dont le corps est un coco traversé par un baton qui lui sert de manche, et auquel est attachée une seule corde de laiton tendue par une cheville; corde sur laquelle, par la pression alternée du doigt, ils tirent deux sons variés avec un archet, espèce de petit arc; et l'*oricongo* enfin, que je représente ici" (the Benguela and Angolan Blacks should be cited as more the musicians, and are above all remarkable for their industrious manufacturing of instruments such as the *marimba, viola* of Angola, a sort of four-stringed lyre; the *violin,* the body of which is a coconut crossed by a stick that serves as a handle, and which is attached to a single string stretched by a brass ankle rope on which, by the alternating pressure of the finger, they derive two various sounds with a bow, kind of a small arc, and finally *oricongo,* which I represent here).

About lamellophones which Debret also illustrates in several of his paintings he writes: "Le *marimba,* espèce d'harmonica, se compose de lames de fer fixées sur une planchette de bois, et soutenues par un chevalet. Chacune de ces lames vibre en échappant à la pression des pouces du joueur, qui les force à fléchir, et produit un son harmonique.... Une portion d'énorme calebasse, approchée de la table d'harmonie de cet instrument, lui prête un son beaucoup plus grave et à peu près semblable à celui d'une harpe" (The Marimba, a kind of harmonica, consists of iron plates attached to a wooden board, and supported by an easel. Each of these blades vibrates by escaping from the pressure of the player's thumbs, which forces them to bend and produces a harmonic sound.... A huge portion of calabash, approached from the soundboard of the instrument, lends it a much deeper sound and somewhat similar to that of a harp).

David Thiermann discussed the subject of Brazilian lamellophones in a letter-article to the editor of the journal *African Music*.[93] He wonders why lamellophones have virtually disappeared in Brazil, while they were so popular in nineteenth century Rio de Janeiro.

I suspect that some of the same causes which led to the decrease of lamellophone playing in Central and East Africa could have been at work in Brazil as well: the introduction of modern transport which made fewer people perform long journeys on foot, and therefore also eliminated the need for a pastime instrument during the walks; the terrible noise in modern cities through motor traffic would make the soft-voiced lamellophones simply unheard. A third factor could have been the increasing availability of guitars to the Black population with the changing economic situation. In Central Africa during the postwar economic boom (1950-1966) the "dry" guitar became the "successor" of a specific type of lamellophone. Sometimes tunes and playing styles were transferred directly from the lamellophone to the guitar.[94] It is possible, therefore, that echoes of the past lamellophone music live on in some rural Brazilian guitar styles even today.

In 1975 I launched a public inquiry concerning lamellophones in Brazil.[95] As a result of various investigations some new data about African-Brazilian lamellophones emerged. The young Brazilian musicologist José Jorge de Carvalho, of the Centro Nacional de Referência Cultural, Universidade Nacional de Brasília, has recently brought to light that lamellophones must have existed in Rio de Janeiro as late as the 1930s. He sent me a surprising photograph of two specimens described as "Instrumentos Musicais Afro-Brasileiros."[96] I have been able to identify one of them as a type known in eastern Angola as *chisandzi cha lungandu* (Ngangela language) or *mandumbwa* (Chokwe language). This is a board-type lamellophone with 12 lamellae arranged in two rows (two "manuals"). Should it really be a Brazilian-made specimen and not perhaps an unfortunate turn-up from some African collection, its presence in Brazil would confirm that a substantial number of people from *far* inland Angola were deported to Brazil, from the country of the Ngangela, Chokwe, Luvale and Lunda in the east. This is what is said about the slave trade in oral traditions I collected among the Luchazi (a Ngangela subgroup) in 1971.

Another lamellophone said to be Brazilian is kept in the Schwarz collection of the Vienna Ethnographic Museum (Museum für Völkerkunde). It is of a type totally different from any of those we have studied above. It belongs to a group which was classified by Jean-Sebastian Laurenty as "Sanza type LOANGO," a lamellophone with a bell-shaped resonator, *only* found on the Loango coast (Cabinda, Congo-Brazzaville, Congo) and in adjacent areas. The Vienna specimen which is still in excellent condition was collected by Schwarz in the first half of the nineteenth century. Schwarz was Consul of the United States in Vienna from 1827-1848. He died in 1867. Eventually his collection of ethnographica mainly from North America was acquired by the Museum für Völkerkunde, Vienna. Unfortunately, due to the absence of any documentation about this specimen of lamellophone, its Brazilian provenance has not yet been fully ascertained.[97]

Another illustration by Alexandre Rodrigues Ferreira (1783-1792) depicts a bow-lute described as "Viola q. tocão os Pretós" (Guitar which the Blacks play) (Fig. 31). No African name is given.

Fig. 31. "Viola q. tocão os Pretós" (Viola that is played by the Blacks). Drawing of a bow-lute found in northern Brazil in the late eighteenth century. This is a type which originated in southwestern Angola, where it is still popular today. Only the hands of the players and the red sleeves of his jacket or uniform are shown in this picture. The instrument was held horizontally while playing, the bows pointing away from the body. A string attached near the orifice of the shovel-shaped resonator served for carrying the instrument. It was obviously often played walking. Reproduced from Alexandre Rodrigues Ferreira's *Viagem Filosófica...* (1783-1792). Courtesy of Biblioteca National, Rio de Janeiro.

In Africa bow-lutes (also called pluriarcs) are found today in a major part of Congo.[98] They have also been reported from Benin where they were already present on seventeenth century bronze plaques and they occur in the western third of Angola.[99] In 1692 Merolla included a four-string bow-lute in his famous illustration, reporting the name *nsambi*. This is the correct spelling. The same name reappears in Cuba as we know from Fernando Ortiz' monumental work.[100] It is also reported from Rio de Janeiro in the nineteenth century under the Englishman's spelling *sambee* by Lieutenant Chamberlain, who mentions a "Congo Negro" who "is performing a different tune upon the Sambee, an instrument of his country" (Fig. 32).[101]

Fig. 32. Lieutenant Chamberlain's illustration, "Sick Negroes" (reproduced from *Views and Costumes of the City and Neighborhood of Rio de Janeiro, Brazil...* London, 1822). The accompanying text says: "In early Morning, but more usually about Sun-set, Parties of newly-imported invalid Negroes are seen taking the Air, in the Suburbs, under the care of a Capataz, or Keeper, who generally bears the Badge of his office—a Whip—more for show than use. These miserable Creatures, actually reduced to Skin and Bone, have the appearance of scarecrows, and it is sometimes extraordinary how such emaciated beings can muster sufficient strength to walk about. The other two Negroes, totally unconcerned at the passing scene, and inattentive to everything but their Musick, to which, as well as dancing and Finery, they are all passionately given, are pursuing their way. One a Native of Moçambique, playing under the rude instrument of his country, called the Madimba, a sort of violin with a single Wire; whilst the other, a Congo Negro, is performing a different tune upon the Sam-

bee, an instrument of his country. Native Airs are generally preferred by them to all others, and when these instruments are in the hands of Proficients, the Musick they are made to produce is by no means unpleasing." Courtesy of Biblioteca Nacional, Rio de Janeiro.

Debret also reports the presence of a four-string bow-lute in Rio de Janeiro. He does not give any African name but describes it as "la *viole d'Angola,* espèce de lyre à quatre cordes" (the viola of Angola, a sort of four-stringed lyre).[102]

The type of bow-lute drawn by Ferreira finds its counterpart in none of the African areas mentioned by the other authors, but in southwestern Angola, in the hinterland of the port of Benguela. When I studied there in 1965 it was still a most popular instrument played by old and young people alike. I noted the Humbi and Handa name *chihumba.* This type of bow-lute is different in its construction from the Congo and West African specimens. The *chihumba* is what Ferreira drew in his picture (Fig. 33).

Fig. 33. Bow-lutes in southwestern Angola, 1965. The two instruments belonged to Chief Arturo Branco, of village Mambondwe (Circunscrição Dinde/Quiiengues), who was himself an excellent player of the *chihumba* (bow-lute). The people in this village are Vahanda, speaking Luhanda language. Photo by Gerhard Kubik, southwestern Angola, July 23, 1965.

I recorded a great number of bow-lute players in that area in 1965. My photograph of Uzavela from Mukondo (Dinde/Quilengues) shows how Ferreira's type of bow-lute has lived on in southwestern Angola until the present time (Fig. 34). The instrument of Uzavela as all the others I recorded can be compared in nearly every detail to the late eighteenth century Brazilian document. Only the number of strings is different, eight for Uzavela and seven for Ferreira's African musician in northern Brazil. Uzavela's playing position should give a fair idea about how the Angolan-originated bow-lute was played in northern Brazil in Ferreira's time, in spite of the enormous time difference.

Fig. 34. Uzavela, aged ca. 18, with his *chihumba* (bow-lute) during a walk through the plantation of Mukondo, ca. 10 km from Mambondwe (Circunscrição Dinde/Quiiengues, southwestern Angola). Characteristic is the clothing style of the musician with loin cloth and a broad belt. He also wears a comb in his hair, as it was fashionable among young men in Angola in 1965. Uzavela worked on the same plantation as the musical bow player Virasanda. Photo by Gerhard Kubik, Angola, July 25, 1965.

May I suggest for future investigations that some Brazilian cultural scientist, historian, musicologist or anthropologist try to set out on a "historical expedition" following some of the paths of Alexandre Rodrigues Ferreira's journey and see what he can find there in the rural areas of northern Brazil today? It may be useful to keep in mind that African cultural traits (including musical instruments) have often migrated off into the Amerindian population. The most apparent example is the *marimba* xylophone of Guatemala. It could well be that Angolan-originated lamellophones or bow-lutes are played today somewhere in the interior of Brazil by members of Amerindian communities. David Thiermann said that "an old German musician now living in Rio claimed that he saw Brazilian Indians living in the interior town of Goiana near Brasilia, the capital of Brazil, playing the mbira ten years ago."[103]

For the study of African cultures in Brazil and indeed for African diaspora studies in general, it will be a most fruitful experience for any local research worker if he can secure help from Africa in the form of an African cultural scientist or devoted coworker from one of those African regions that were linked with the Americas, and do the field-work jointly, as I did with Donald Kachamba in 1974.

METHODOLOGICAL CONSIDERATIONS

For the tracking down of Angolan traits in Brazilian musical cultures I approached the subject from the following methodological starting points. On the whole, it was found useful to pay attention to the methodology developed by ethno-historians for the comparative historical study of cultures. This does not need special discussion here, as it has been discussed by various authors.[104] Ethnohistory uses written, including pictorial, and oral source material. One of its objectives is to reconstruct the history of peoples and their cultures, even long-term developments, through the chronological "stringing" of a tight *sequence of sources.*

Cultural phenomena are not merely products of historical accidents, however. There are regularities in culture as in any aspect of human behavior. If we had to wait in each case for the discovery of historical records in order to establish the life cycle and trends of specific cultural phenomena, their diffusion and cross-cultural relations, we would wait idly for a long time.

Under favorable conditions it is possible, therefore, to compare with good results *synchronous* material, such as present-day field recordings and pictures and project the results of such comparisons back into history. This is possible whenever there is good reason on the basis of extra-historical (i.e., structural, sociological or psychological) evidence, that the traits to be compared have displayed a certain "historical inertia," that they have tended to resist change for one or the other reason, in the music of Black Africa it is possible to isolate a few elements which seem to show a high degree of historical stability for musico-structural reasons. In the triangle of our comparative research, Angola, Nigeria and Brazil, time-line patterns were named as a very stable element, besides others.

Reasonable historical stability can also be expected in some linguistic traits, since language elements do not change as fast as musical fashions. Some keywords from Angolan and West African languages and terms relating to music and dance were integrated into African-Brazilian terminology. Though they were adapted in their phonetics and often semantics to fit into the pattern of Brazilian Portuguese, their African origins can be detected. For the purpose of tracing African words found in the Americas back to the suspected African languages it was found necessary first to retranscribe them in a Bantu or West African orthography; for example, *quimbanda* as *kimbanda, cuica* as *kwika, ganzá* as *nganza,* or tentatively *capoeira* as *kapwera.* For West African languages phonetic symbols should be used.

It is not possible, however, to compile a comprehensive catalogue of "stable elements" in African musical cultures, because nothing is by nature absolutely stable, and the danger is always that someone in the end makes a dogma out of it. There are only trends and likelihoods; even the time-line patterns can become unstable under very powerful alien influences. What has been discussed in the main text of the book might perhaps unlock a few fruitful areas into which the student of African cultures in the Americas may want to direct his search. And this is the purpose.

In addition to historical inertia for musico-structural or linguistic reasons, there is the inertia in human social behavior itself. It has often been said that musical traditions live and die with their extra-musical social context and that cult music such as *Candomblé* and other religious music is much more stable than entertainment music. This is now commonplace and it may indeed be so in many instances. But stability or change is always the result of an interplay of many factors, and though it is useful to single out a few, in his or her actual scientific performance the researcher will often begin the game with probabilities. He or she will put on his or her screen little units of possible evidence, rearrange them, see whether other units fit, until something like a trend or picture emerges. Then he or she will look out for a possible contradictory picture. Quite often a whole set has to be thrown away and a new one put in.

Some components of a cultural heritage can also be transmitted *unconsciously* between individuals and, ultimately, from generation to generation. It would require considerably more space to explain theoretically how this works, and how it struck me first during field-work in Black Africa. A certain alertness to the possibility of unconscious transmission in culture has also influenced my movements in Brazil. In brief, a trait sometimes disappears from the surface of a specific culture for a certain historical period, for fifty or a hundred years, including all verbal (oral) references to it. After some time, however, when circumstances are favorable and a need arises (for instance, as a result of incisive social changes, or a war situation) the lost trait is "reinvented." The fact is that in such cases *something* was still transmitted all the time, probably a syndrome of interrelated behavioral patterns which *also* contain in a condensed form (like on a micro-film) the possibility of a novel manifestation of the "lost" trait.

In a time of slavery and oppression some specific cultural traits may be forced to disappear among their carriers. They do not really disappear. They only *retreat* to a safer area of the human psyche. For example, if you prosecute drumming in an African community and even burn all the drums of the people, what will happen? The drums will perhaps really disappear and the drum patterns will not be sounded again, but they will still remain—in a silent shape. The drum patterns will just retreat into the body of the people. And there inside they will remain like on a micro-film. This has nothing to do with genetics, because the transmission is cultural, through human interaction. The drum patterns will be transformed into a set of *motional behavior*; they will go back to their source. In this form they will continue to be transmitted from mothers and grandmothers to their children, from father to son during work, non-verbally, as an *awareness* of a style of moving. When a favorable moment in history comes, the drum patterns surface again, perhaps on some other instruments. Some young people suddenly "invent" something new.

The implication is that probably in the Americas there is a lot of African cultural material beneath the surface on such "micro-films." Its presence can be discovered by a variety of methods; one is an adapted psychoanalytical approach, involving friendly people with whom the researcher has very close personal relations into *deep conversation*. In my experience children are usually superb partners in such playful "deep conversations" including acting out dramatically some of the topics that occur.

Out of pure curiosity and interest to know what would happen I submitted some of my Brazilian friends to what I call a *cultural comprehension test*. A "test person" was exposed to musical materials from selected areas in Angola or West Africa, for instance a record, a musical instrument or a syllabic pattern, without his being aware of a test situation. I know that Western moral standards would term this unfair; but actually throughout our human lives we are testing other human beings without their slightest awareness. Children already test their parents, they "try them out," later you test your marriage partner all the time though you never declare it as tests.

I did not create a laboratory situation with my Brazilian friends. The purpose of the comprehension tests was to obtain a *cultural profile* of the tested person. For instance, in one such situation, I put an Angolan lamellophone in front of one of my major informants in Bahia, Vicente dos Santos, on the table before us, while continuing to talk about something else. It was a box-resonated type to be played with thumbs. The idea was that Vicente would react in some way to the presence of this instrument; either "positively" by *understanding* it, or negatively. Vicente's hands really approached the instrument soon, and he began to strike the notes, while I continued deliberately to talk about a different subject. I observed how he was striking: he used his two index fingers, holding the instrument upside down, as one plays the Cuban *marimbula* or the related *agidigbo* of the Yorùbá and Fon. Thus he had reacted *negatively* from the viewpoint of Angolan musical cultures, where this instrument is exclusively played with thumbs. His unconscious had not "understood" this Angolan instrument, and therefore he earned a minus mark for Angola, but a plus mark for Western Nigeria and Cuba, because he had understood it that way. Vicente's cultural profile obtained from *several* informal comprehension tests with him shows a nearly 50:50 distribution of plus marks for Angola and Western Nigeria and Cuba. The latter two components could not be separated in this test set.

Vicente shares both a West African (Yorùbá) and an Angolan cultural heritage.

It is significant, on the other hand, that in Rio de Janeiro almost everybody struck my lamellophone with the *thumbs* in the right playing position. Some people were undecided, but no one struck it in the *marimbula* way. Lamellophones have been absent in Rio for decades, and nobody, except one informant, Lygia Carvalho, did remember having ever seen or heard of such an instrument. Still, this reaction! For comparison, in Central Europe, elderly women in particular often thought that my lamellophone was a mouse-trap! They did not even recognize it as a musical instrument.

Cultural comprehension tests are based on the experience that understanding of cultural objects, traits, etc., is in itself determined by cultural heritage. How a person understands and what he understands constitutes an expression of his cultural profile. Cultural understanding often works as an unconscious process; the tested person may be largely unaware of his true cultural heritage.

SELECT BIBLIOGRAPHY

Some Classic Works on African Cultures in Brazil

Almeida, Renato, *História da música brasileira*, Rio de Janeiro, F. Briguiet, 1926.

—. *Música folclórica e música popular*, IBECC, Comissão Nacional de Folclore, Rio de Janeiro, 1958.

Alvarenga, Oneyda, *Música popular brasileira*, O Globo, Porto Alegre, 1950.

Andrade, Mário de, *Danças dramáticas do Brasil*, Liv. Martins, São Paulo, 1968.

—. *Ensaio sobre música brasileira*, Liv. Martins, São Paulo, 1968.

Araújo, A. Maynard, *Documentário folclórico paulista*, Departamento de Cultura, São Paulo, 1952.

Azevedo, Fernando, *A cultura brasileira*, E. Nacional, São Paulo, 1954.

Azevedo, Thales, *Cultura e situação racial no Brasil*, Civilização Brasileira, Rio de Janeiro, 1966.

Bastide, Roger, *La batuque de Pòrto Alegre,* University of Chicago Press, New York, Chicago, 1959.

—. *O candomblé da Bahia,* Ed. Nacional, São Paulo, 1961.

—. *Estudos afro-brasileiras.* Universidade de São Paulo, FFCL, 1953.

—. *Sociologia do folclore brasileiro,* Anhembi, São Paulo, 1959.

Bittencourt, Gastão de, *O folklore no Brasil,* Progresso, Salvador, 1957.

Cardoso, Fernando H., *Capitalismo e escravidão no Brasil meridional. O negro na sociedade escravocrata do Rio Grande do Sul,* Difusão Européia do Livro, Sâo Paulo, 1962.

Carneiro, A. J. de Souza, *Os mitos qfricanos no Brasil,* Cia. Ed. Nacional, São Paulo, 1937.

Carneiro, Edison, *Antologia do negro brasileiro,* Ed. Globo, Porto Alegre, 1950.

—. *Candomblés da Bahia,* Secretaria da Educação e Saúde, 1948.

—. *Guerra de los palmares,* Fondo de la Cultura Económica, México, 1940.

—. *Ladinos e crioulos: estudo sobre o negro no Brasil,* Ed. Civilização Brasileira, Rio de Janeiro, 1964.

—. *Negros bantus,* Ed. Civilização Brasileira, Rio de Janeiro, 1937.

—. *O Quilombo de Palmares,* Cia. Ed. Nacional, São Paulo, 1958.

—.*Samba de umbigada*, Cia. de Defesa do Folclore Brasileiro, Rio de Janeiro, 1961.

Cascudo, Luís da Camara, *Dicionário do folclore brasileiro*, MEC, Rio de Janeiro, 1954.

Costa, E. Viotti, *Da senzala à colònia*, Difusão Europeia do Livro, São Paulo, 1966.

Couty, Louis, *L'esclavage au Brésil*, Guillaumin e Cie., Paris, 1881.

Diégues, Manuel Jr., *População e açúcar no nordeste*, Casa do Estudante do Brasil, 1959.

Fernandes, Florestan, *Folklore e mudança social na cidade de São Pauio*, Ahnembi, São Paulo, 1961

—. *The negro in Brazilian society*, Columbia University Press, New York, 1969.

Freitas, Newton, *Macumba*, Guaíra, Curitiba, 1949.

Freitas, Otávio, *Doenças qfricanas no Brasil*, Ed. Nacional, São Paulo, 1935.

Freyre, Gilberto, *Casa grande e senzala*, Liv. José Olympio Ed., Rio de Janeiro, 1952.

—. *New world in the tropics*, Knopf, New York, 1959.

—. *Problemas brasileiros de antropologia*, Casa do Estudante do Brasil, Rio de Janeiro, 1943.

Harris, Marvin, *Town and country in Brazil*, Columbia University Press, New York, 1956.

Herskoits, M. J., *Pesquisas etnológicas na Bahia,* Sociedade Brasileira de Antropologìa e Etnologia, Publicação do Museu do Estado da Bahia, 1942.

Ianni, Octavio, *Raças e classes sociais no Brasil,* Ed. Civilização Brasileira, Rio de Janeiro, 1966.

Johnston, Harry, *The Negro in the New World,* Macmillan Co., New York, 1910.

Kazadi Wa Mukuna, *O contato musical transatlântico: Contribuição Bantu na música popular brasileira.* Tese de doutoramento em Sociologia, Departamento de Ciências Sociais da Faculdade de Filosofia, Letras e Ciências Humanas da Universidade de São Paulo. [Resumo de Tese: *Africa,* Revista do Centro de Estudos Africanos da USP, No. 1 (1), 1978.]

Kleppenburg, Boaventura, *A umbanda no Brasil,* E. Vozes, Petrópolis, 1961.

Lima, Vicente, *Xangó,* Divulgação do Centro de Cultura Afro-Brasileira, Recife, 1937.

Malheiros, A. M. P., *A Escravidão no Brasil: ensaio histórico, jurídico e social,* Ed. Cultural, São Paulo, 1964.

Melo, Antônio da Silva, *Estudos sobre o negro,* José Olympio, Rio de Janeiro, 1958.

Moraes, Evaristo de, *A escravidão africana no Brasil,* Ed. Nacional, São Paulo, 1934.

Mortara, Giorgio, *A composição da população segundo a côr no Brasil,* IBGE, Rio de Janeiro, 1947.

Nascimento, Abdias, *O negro revoltado,* Ed. G. R. D.t Rio de Janeiro, 1968.

Netto, Antônio da Silva, *Segundos estudos sobre a emancipação dos escravos no Brasil*, Rio de Janeiro, 1968.

Ortiz, Oderigo N. R., *La presencia del negro en la mùsica del Brasil*, Buenos Aires, 1969.

Peixe, Cesar Guerra, *Maracatùs do Recife*, Ricordi, São Paulo, 1955.

Pereira, Manuel Numes, *Negros escravos na Amazônia*, Marajó, Souré, 1943.

Pierson, Donald, *Os africanos da Bahia*, Departamento de Cultura, São Paulo, 1941.

—. *O candomblé da Bahia*, Guaira, Curitiba, 1942.

—. *Cruz das Almas: a Brazilian village*, Smithsonian Institute Publications, No. 12, Washington, 1951.

Pinto, L. A. da Costa, *O negro no Rio de Janeiro*, Ed. Nacional, São Paulo, 1954.

Porter, Dorothy B., *Afro-Braziliana, a working bibliography*, G. K. Hall & Co., Boston, Mass., 1978.

Pradez, Charles, *Nouvelles études sur le Brésil*, Thorin, Paris, 1872.

Querino, Manuel, *A arte culinária na Bahia*, Lív. Progresso, Salvador, 1954.

—. *Costumes africanos no Brasil*, Civilização Brasileira, Rio de Janeiro, 1938.

Ramos, Arthur, *Aculturação negra no Brasil*, Cia. Ed. Nacional, São Paulo, 1942.

—. *As culturas negras no novo mundo,* Civilização Brasileira, Rio de Janeiro, 1937.

—. *O folclore negro no Brasil,* Liv. Casa do Estudante do Brasil, Rio de Janeiro, 1954.

—. *Negros bantus no Brasil,* Conferência na Sociedade Luso-Africana do Rio de Janeiro, Julho 22, 1936.

—. *The negro in Brazil,* The Associated Publishers, Washington, 1938.

—. *O negro na civilização brasileira,* Conferência no Centro Oswald Spengler, da Faculdade de Direito do Rio de Janeiro, 25 de Novembro de 1933.

Ribeiro, Joaquim, *Folklore baiano,* MEC, Rio de Janeiro, 1956.

Ribeiro, M. J. Borges, *A dança do Moçambique,* Ed. Ricordi, São Paulo, 1960.

Ribeiro, René, *Cultos afro-brasileiros do Recife: um estudo de ajustamento social,* Instituto Joaquim Nabuco de Pesquisas Sociais, Recife, 1952.

Rodrigues, J. Honório, *Brasil e África,* Civilização Brasileira, 1961.

Rodrigues, Nina, *Os africanos no Brasil,* Ciá. Ed, Nacional, São Paulo, 1945.

Santos, Descoredes M., *Contos negros da Bahia,* Ed. G. R. D., Rio de Janeiro, 1961.

Souza, Carneiro, *Mitos Africanos do Brasil,* Cia. Ed. Nacional, Sâo Paulo, 1961.

Sparta, Francisco, *A dança dos Orixás,* Ed. Herder, Sâo Paulo, 1970.

Tannebaum, F., *El negro en las Americas: esclavo y ciudadano,* Paidos, Buenos Aires, 1968.

Valente, Valdemar, *Sobrevivências dahomeanas nos grupos de culto afro-nordestinos,* Instituto Joaquim Nabuco de Pesquisas Sociais, Recife, 1964.

Verger, Pierre, *Notes sur le culte des Orisa et Voâun,* Ifan, Dakar, 1975.

—. *Flux et reflux de la traite des nègres entre le golfe de Bénin et Bahia de Todos os Santos du dix-septième au dix-neuvième siècle,* Mouton, Paris, 1968.

Waglev, Charles, *An introduction to Brazil,* Columbia University Press, New York, 1963.

NOTES

1. Johann Moritz Rugendas, *Malerische reise in Brasilien* (Paris: Engelmann, 1835), 28-29.

2. "Vissungo" (braz.) is a word found in languages of Eastern Angola, such as Ngangela. It just means "songs." The singular is *chisungo*, the plural *visungo*. Many writers, unaware of the meaning of this word, made a "double plural" out of it introducing the form *"vissungos."* See "Negro Work Songs of the Diamond District in Minas Gerais, Brazil," in *Music in the Americas*, ed. G. List and Juan Orrego-Salas (Bloomington: Indiana University, 1967).

3. Fernando Augusto Albuquerque Mourão, *La contribution de l'Afrique Bantoue à la formation de la société brésilienne: une tentative de redéfinition méthodologique* (Centro de estudos Africanos, Universidade de Sao Paulo, 1974).

4. Compare also David Clement Scott and Alexander Hetherwick, *Dictionary of the Chichewa language* (Malawi: C.L.A.I.M., Blantyre, 1929 [1970]).

5. An impressive coverage of the Carnival is found in Marcel Camus' film *Orfeo Negro*, made in Rio de Janeiro in 1958 as a French/Italian/Brazilian coproduction. Director: Marcel Camus. Camera: Jean Bourgoin. Music: Luis Bonfa, Antonio Carlos Johim. Cast: Breno Mello, Marpessa Dawn, Adhemar da Silva, Lourdes de Oliveira. Production,: Dispatfilm/Gemma, Cinematográfica, Tupan Filmes, 105 min, Eastman Color, Cinemascope.

6. For more details about *agogo in* Yoruba culture of southwestern Nigeria, see Jerome O. Ojo, *Yoruba Customs from Ondo* (Vienna: Acta Ethnologica et Linguistica, No. 37, Series Africana 10, 1976), 89.

7. Compare our recordings, Kachamba and Kubik, Salvador, October 1974, tapes V 2/II and V 4/I, copied in the Phonogrammarchiv, Vienna; further the recordings of the Herskovits collection of 1941, Library of Congress; and the record Brésil, vol. 2, by Simone Dreyfus-Roche, 1955, published by the Musée de l'Homme, Paris.

8. J.H. Kwabena Nketia: *The music of Africa*, London, Victor Gollancz, Ltd., 1975, 131.

9. Gerard Kubik, "Oral notation of some west and central African time-line patterns", *Review of Ethnology*, Vol. 3, No. 2, 1972.

10. Gerhard Kubik, "Transmission et transcription des éléments de musique instrumentale africaine," *Bulletin of the International Committee on Urgent Anthropological and Ethnological Research*, No. 11, 1969; idem, "Oral notation...," *Review of Ethnology*, Vol. 3, No. 22, 1972; idem, "Verstehen in afrikanischen Musikkulturen," in Peter Fultin und Hans-Peter Reinecke (Hrsg.), *Musik und Verstehen: Aufsätze zur semiotischen Theorie, Asthetik and Sociologie der musikalischen Rezeption* (Köln: Arno Volk Veriag—Hans Gerig KG, 1973), 171-188.

11. Laz E.N. Ekwueme, "Structural levels of rhythm and form in African Music with particular reference to the West Coast," *African Music*, Vol. 5, No. 4, 1975/6, 30-32.

12. Compare recordings Kachamba and Kubik of 1974, Phonogrammarchiv, Vienna.

13. A.M. Jones, *African Music in Northern Rhodesia and some other places*, The Occasional Papers of the Rhodes-Livingstone Museum, Livingstone (Zambia), 1949, 12-14. Jones dealt with it extensively in his study of Bemba music in Zambia See recordings Kubik of 1964, 1966 and 1969, Central African Republic and Cameroon, Phonogrammarchiv, Vienna.

14. Recording B 10 143/Kubik, Angola 1965, Phonogrammarchiv, Vienna.

15. Field-notes Kubik, 1965, in Angola, and 1971 and 1973, in northwestern Zambia.

16. David Rycroft, "The Guitar improvisations of Mwenda Jean Bosco" (parts I and II), *African Music*, Vol. 2, No. 4; Vol. 3, No. 1, 1961-1962.

17. Kazadi wa Mukuna, "Trends of Nineteenth and twentieth Century Music in the Congo-Zaïre," in Robert Günther, *Musikkulturen Asiens, Afrikas und Ozianiens im 19. Jahrhundert* (Regensberg: Bosse, 1973), 273.

18. See also Emil Pearson, *People of the Aurora* (San Diego: Beta Books, 1977), 157. My co-worker Mose Yotuma from northwestern Zambia says that this word is usually used with reference to animals, especially antelopes. "Vambambi vekusamba ngwe kuli kalunga wamundende" (the duikers jump when there is little rain). He also says that in eastern Angola and northwestern Zambia there is an old dance called Sambakalata (Interview, Dec. 3, 1978).

19. Paul Olivier, *Savannah Syncopaters: African Retentions in the Blues* (New York: Stein and Day, 1970). See also the discussion of Oliver's thesis by G.Kubik, in *Jazzforschung/Jazz research*, III, Graz, 1970, 164-66; Lynn Summers, Paul Oliver and David Evans, in *Living Blues*, No. 6, Autumn 1971, 30-36, No. 8, Spring 1972, 13-17, No.10, Autumn 1972, 27-29, No. 13, Summer 1973, 29-32.

20. Alex Haley, *Roots* (London: Hutchinson & Co. Ltd., 1977).

21. For some recent findings on perceptional and cognitive aspects of African music, see my paper: "Perzeptorische und Kognitive Grundlagen der Musikgestaltung in Schwartzafrica," *Musicologica Austriaca*, No. 1, 1977 (published by Musikwissenchaftliches Insitiut, University of Vienna, Universitätsstrasse 7, A-1010, Vienna).

22. Alan Lomax, Irmgard Bartenieff, Forrestine Paulay, "Choreometrics: a method for the study of cross-cultural patterns in film", *Research Film*, Vol. No. 6, 1969.

23. Alfons M. Dauer, "Stil und Technik in afrikanischen Tanz," *Afrika heute* (Sonderbeilage), No. 24, December 15, 1967.

24. Helmut Günther, *Grundphänomene und Grundbegriffe des afrikanischen und afroamerikanischen Tanzes* (Graz: Beitrage zur Jazzforschung, 1969), 34.

25. Private visit to Evans at Yorba Linda, California, August 1977.

26. Tape A 1/1, Salvador, Sept. 18, 1975, copied in Phonogrammarchiv, Vienna.

27. Recordings Kubik, October 1975, Tape No. A. 2/1 and II, copied at the Phonogrammarchiv, Vienna.

28. For more details, see Gerard Kubik, *Mehrstimmigkeit und Tonsysteme in Zentral- und Ostafrika* (Vienna, 1968); idem, "Likembe tunings of Kufuna Kandonga, Angola," *African Music*, Vol. 6, No. 1, 1977.

29. See: Rossini Tavares de Lima, *Folclore de São Paulo (Melodia e Ritmo)* (São Paulo: Ricordi, 1954), 122.

30. Lourdes Gonçalves Furtardo, "The Carimbo—A dance of Salgado zone, Pará, Brazil," *Review of Ethnology*, Vol. 5-7, 1977.

31. Compare Veiga de Oliveira's book on Portuguese musical instruments. Ernesto Veiga de Oliveira, *Instrumentos Musicais populares Portugueses* (Lisboa: Fundaçao Calouste Gulbenkian, 1966), 314-324.

32. Heinz Weischoff, *Die Afrikanischen Trommeln und ihre ausserafrikanischen Beziehungen* (Frankfurt, 1933).

33. See Angola recordings Kubik 1965, in the Phonogrammarchiv, Vienna, and record published at Tervuren.

34. Tape 51, at Quicuco, July 13, 1965.

35. Jean-Sebastian Laurenty, "Les membranophones des Luba-Shankadi," *African Music*, Vol. 5, No. 2, 1972, 44-45.

36. See Angola recordings Kubik, in the Phonogrammarchiv, Vienna; copies of the Angola tape collection are found in the Instituto de Investigação Cientifica de Angola, Luanda.

37. Interview, Dec. 3, 1978.

38. A useful analysis of "magico-religious" terms in various Angolan languages and their geographical distribution can be found in M.L. Rodrigues de Areira, "Estrutura mágico-religiosa de uma trilogia tradi-

cional nas populacoes de Angola," in *Memoriam Antonio Jorge Dias*, III (Lisboa: Instituto de Alta Cultura, Junta de Invstiga⊠oes Cientificas do Ultramar, 1974).

39. See also recordings of mahamba sessions Kubik/Angola 1965, Tape 77/ II, Kusa-Chingangu; Kubik/Zambia 1971, Tapes L 1 and L 2, Chikenge; in the Phono- grammarchiv, Vienna; unpublished ciné-films in private archive Kubik, Vienn.

40. Gerard Kubik, *Die Institution mukandaund assoziierte Einrichtungen bei den Vambwela/Vankangela und verwandten Ethnien in Sudostangola*. Field research document, August-December, 1965. Dissertation, University of Vienna).

41. Candido Emanuel Felix, *A Cartilha da Umbanda* (Rio de Janeiro: Editora Eco, 1972).

42. See, for instance, Lourenço Braga, *Umbanda e magia branca, Quimbanda e magia negra* (Rio de Janeiro: Edições Spiker, 1961); António de Alva, *Como desmanchar trabalhos de Quimbanda (Magia Negra)*, vol. II (Rio de Janeiro: Editorio Eco, 1970); Oliveira Magno, *Ritual prático de Umbanda* (Rio de Janeiro: Editoria Espiritualista, 1961).

43. Onyeda Alvarenga, *Musica popular brasileña* (Buenos Aires, 1974), 132. This text is the Spanish edition of Alvarenga's book.

44. See, for instance, Araújo in his *Cultura popular brasileira*, São Paulo, 1973, 135.

45. Waldeloir Rego, *Capoeira Angola: Ensaio Sócio-Etnográfico* (Rio de Janeiro: Editôra Itapuá, Coleção Baiana, 1968).

46. From oral traditions collected in Salvador, 1975.

47. From oral traditions collected in Salvador, 1975.

48. Conversation in Vienna, April 1977.

49. Compare also David Rycroft, "The new 'town music' of southern Africa," *Recorded Folk Music*, Vol.1, Sept./Oct. 1958.

50. One item is published on my record *Humbi et Handa – Angola*, Musée Royal de l'Afrique Centrale, Tervuren, 1973, side B/1 (*okutanta*). Other

items are found under Kubik/Angola recordings, 1965, in the Phonogrammarchiv, Vienna.

51. Rugendas, *Malerische*, 26.

52. See the list in Waldeloir Rego, pp. 27-29.

53. For a general discussion, see R. K. Kent, "Palmares: An African State in Brazil" and Stuart B. Schwartz, "The Mocambo: Slave Resistance in Colonial Bahia," reprinted in Richard Price, ed., *Maroon Societies: Rebel Slave Communities in the Americas* (New York: Anchor Books, 1973).

54. See the record published in Tervuren, Side B, No. 4, "Chirumba chetu."

55. Debret's pictures are found in the museum of the Fundação Raymundo Ottoni de Castro Maya, in Rio de Janeiro. I am very grateful to Mrs. Julia Olinto, Superintendent, for allowing me to take photographs of the pictures of Debret and other painters.

56. Jean-Baptiste Debret, *Voyage pittoresque et historique au Brésil, au Séjour d'un artiste francais au Brésil dépuis 1816 jusqu'en 1831 inclusivement* (Paris, 1834), 39, 129.

57. Lieutnant Chamberlain , *Views and costumes of the city and neighbourhood of Rio de Janeiro, Brazil, 1819-1820* (London, 1822).

58. See also Ferdinand J. de Hen, *Beitrag zur Kenntis der Musikinstrumente aus Belgisch-Kongo und Ruanda-Urundi* (Köln, 1960), 36-37.

59. This is the full name of the type of bow used in *Capoeira* today. I know of four types of *berimbau* in Brazil. This is the terminology: *berimbau de barriga* (the gourd-resonated bow), *berimba de boca* (either a mouthbow or a jew's harp), and *berimbau de bacia*. I did not see the last mentioned variety myself. Senhor Descartes Cadelha, a Brazilian painter, saw it 30 km outside of the city of Fortaleza. The resonator is a hand-basin *(bacia)* squeezed between the bow and its string. The musician holds his instrument in *vertical* position like a string-bass, sitting on a chair. For changing the pitch he uses a bottle as a slider, holding it in its left hand. In his right hand he holds the stick for striking the string. What I am describing here I am deducing from a drawing Senhor Descartes made for me.

60. See Tony Talbot's film *Berimbau*, 16mm, colour, New Yorker Films, 1971.

61. See my Tervuren record.

62. Fernando Ortiz, *Los instrumentos de la musica afro-cubana*, vol. 5 (Habana, 1952), 21.

63. See Waldeloir Rego, pp. 74-76.

64. Malawi field-notes, 1967.

65. Compare the Brazilian pictures in this book with those of the Angolan counterparts. See also Gerhard Kubik, "Musical bows in south-western Angola, 1965," *African Music*, Vol. 4, 1975-6.

66. Field-notes in Tanzania, October-December 1976.

67. See notes to recordings Kubik, Nov. 27, 1963, No. B 8624-25 and B 8626, Phonogrammarchiv, Vienna.

68. See the catalogue by Alfred Janata, *Aussereuropaische Musikinstrumente* (Wien: Museum für Völkerkunde, 1961), 14, particularly the exhibition objects No. 66 421 from Kumba (Cameroon) and No. 136 301 from the Mandara mountains (northeastern Nigeria/northern Cameroon).

69. Encyclopaedia Cinem tographica, No. E 244.

70. An illustration can be found in Araújo, p. 133.

71. Field-notes, Malawi 1967.

72. Field-notes, Angola 1965, Malawi 1967, Tanzania, 1961-62 and 1976.

73. Compare A. M. Jones' interesting remarks on how in the lamellophone playing techniques two imaginary (xylophone) players are merged into one single person (A. M. Jones' letter to the editor of *African Music*, Vol. 5, No. 3, 1973/4).

74. For a general discussion, see my article "Marimba," in the *New Grove's Dictionary of Music and Musicians,* London.

75. George W. Cable, "The Dance in Place Congo," *The Century Magazine*, Vol. 31, February 1886, 571-532.

76. George List, "The musical bow at Palenque," *Journal of the International Folk Music Council*, Vol. XVIII, 1966.

77. Rossini Tavares de Lima, *Folklore de São Paulo* (São Paulo, 1954), 149-150.

78. Henry Koster, *Viagens ao Nordeste do Brasil*. Tradução e notas de Luis de Câmara Cascudo (São Paulo: Companhia Editora Nacional, 1942).

79. For detailed information on xylophones in southern Cameroon, see Pie-Claude Ngumu, *Les mendzan des Chanteurs de Yaoundé: Histioire, organologie, fabrication, système de transcription*, Acta Ethnologica et Linguistica, No. 34, Series Musicologica 2, Vienna, 1976.

80. Field-notes, Cameroon, 1969-1970.

81. Giovanni Antonio Cavazzi, *Istorica Descrizione de' Tre' Regni Congo, Matamba, et Angola* (Bologna, 1687).

82. Girolamo Merolla, *Breve, e svccinia Relatione del viaggio nel regno di Congo nell'Africa Meridionale...* (Napoli, 1692).

83. Walter Hirschberg, "Early historical illustrations of West and Central African music," *African Music*, Vol. 4, No. 3 (1968): 16.

84. Carl Friedrich Phillipp von Martius and Johann Baptist Spix, *Atlas zur Reise in Brasilien* (München: M. Lindauer, 1817-1820).

85. Günther, *Grundphänomene*, 26.

86. Maurice Djenda, "Les anciennes danses des Mpyèmo," *African Music* Vol. 4, No.1 (1966-1967): 44.

87. From the introduction to Ferreira's work by Professor José Candido de Melo Carvalho of the Museu Nacional, Rio de Janeiro, October 20, 1970.

88. See recordings Kubik/southwestern Angola, 1965, player: Docota, at Munengole, Nos. B 10 098 "Elamba" and B 10 099 "O andamento do convoy," Phonogrammarchiv, Vienna.

89. See the list of Angolan lamellophone names I published in *African Music*, Vol. 3, No. 4, 1965.

90. A vivid documentation of what a treasury of oral knowledge Sakapan-dulula was is found in Kayombo ka Chinyeka's booklet, *Vihandyeka vya mana — sayings of wisdom*, Acta Ethnoligica et Linguistica, No. 30, Series Africana 8, Vienna, 1973.

91. Letter by Margot Dias, dated March 6, 1977.

92. Thomas Ewbank, *Life in Brazil, or a journey to the land of the cocoa and the palm* (New York: Harper and Bros., 1856), 111-112.

93. Letters to the Editor, "The mbira in Brazil," *African Music*, Vol. 5, No. 1 (1971): 90-94.

94. See Gerhard Kubik, "Neue Musikformen in Schwartzafrica. Psychologische und musik-ethnologische Grundlagen," *Afrika heute* (Sonderbellage), I.März (1965): 15.

95. Anon., "Quem conhece ainda o lamelophone marimba? Etnólogo austriaco estuda fenómenos culturais afro-brasileiros," *Noticias da Áustria*, No. 2, 1976.

96. Reproduced from the *Boletín Latinoamericano de Música* (Rio de Janeiro), Vol. 6, No. 1 (1964): 149.

97. Gerhard Kubik, "Die 'brasilianische Sanza' im Museum für Völkerkunde Wien", Archiv für Völkerkunde, in press.

98. See Laurenty for distribution. Jean-Sebastian Laurenty, *Les Cordophones du Congo Belge et du Ruanda-Urundi* (Tervuren: Annales du Musée Royal du Congo Belge, 1960).

99. Dan Ben-Amos, *Sweet words: Storytelling events in Benin* (Philadelphia, 1975), 27-28.

100. Ortiz, *Los instrumentos...* (1952), V: 15, 26.

101. See Chamberlain's note on "Sick Negroes," in *Views and customes*.

102. Debret, *Voyage pittoresque*, 129.

103. Thiermann, "The mbira in Brazil," 94. Mbira is a name for some types of lamellophones found in Zimbabwe and adjacent areas. The term is often applied incorrectly by writers to lamellophones never called *mbira* by the members of the musical communities concerned.

104. See, for instance, regular contributions in the journals *Ethnohistory* and *Wiener Ethnohistorische Blätter*, or individual publications such as the well known works of Hirschberg, Sturtevant, Vansina and others: Walter Hirschberg, "Kulturhistorie und Ethnohistorie," in *Mitteilungen zur Kulturkunde*, Bd. 1 (1966); William C. Sturtevant, "Anthropology, History and Ethnohistory," *Ethnohistory*, Vol. 13, No. 1-2 (1966); Jan Vansina, *Oral tradition: A study of historical methodology* (London, 1965).

INDEX

A

Brazilian shanty-towns (*favelas*)   6

C

D

Lightning Source UK Ltd.
Milton Keynes UK
UKOW04f1139010218
317200UK00001B/311/P